THE GIFT OF FAILURE

THE GIFT
OF
FAILURE

ARI RASTEGAR

RASTEGAR

THE GIFT OF FAILURE
Turn My Missteps Into Your Epic Success

FIRST EDITION

ISBN 978-1-5445-3317-9 *Hardcover*
     978-1-5445-3316-2 *Paperback*
     978-1-5445-3315-5 *Ebook*
     978-1-5445-3318-6 *Audiobook*

CONTENTS

INTRODUCTION

"Fail early, fail often, but always fail forward."

—JOHN C. MAXWELL

I hope you fail—and I hope you fail a lot.

That might sound harsh, but I mean it from the depths of my heart. I also want you to find success and fulfillment—and you need to fail in order to do that.

We tend to think everything is good or bad, but failure is amoral. It's simply a universal experience. With perseverance and honest introspection, failure eventually leads to success—they are two sides of the same coin. Innovation inherently requires trial and error; nothing can be created without trying out new concepts. The error is the gift.

In his book, *Failing Forward*, the world-famous author John C. Maxwell says that regardless of how talented or brilliant you are, you *will* encounter failure—it's just a matter of when.

Since failure is inevitable, the real question then becomes *How will you react to it?*

Reacting positively to failure is hard, but like everything, it's a learned skill. Even when you react positively, failure still hurts, but eventually the sting subsides and you grow stronger. Instead of letting failures paralyze us and cause setbacks, we need to acknowledge that they will come, and use them as stepping stones to move forward with confidence.

It has never been easy, but I've learned to use failure as fuel for personal growth, which then translated into business growth. Responding to failure so that it fuels you is a *must*—make it as such. Something magical happens when a *want* turns into a *must*. The universe conspires to make things happen.

Viewed in that light, failing is not just a good thing—it is a necessity.

I like the way Ernest Hemingway explained it: "The world breaks everyone and afterward many are strong at the broken places." Find what is broken and fix it. More importantly, find out *why*. To add to that, Mark Zuckerberg said, "If things aren't breaking, then you're not moving fast enough. People learn by making mistakes."

I humbly admit that I've failed more than I've succeeded. If you aren't doing the same, then you're not challenging yourself enough. If you are an entrepreneur like me, failure is expected. Sadly, we often pretend like it's not. We are taught to value reason above all, so we de-emotionalize work, and we are surprised when things break or when we fail. We pretend it never happened instead of drilling down to learn the painful lessons.

As entrepreneurs, we can and should be emotional, although we hate to admit it. We expect our ideas to turn into products and systems that change the world for the better—that make others happier, healthier, and create value. We aspire to identify a problem, find a solution, and build a company offering that solution. We do this on behalf of our clients to make their lives easier, more convenient, or simply more enjoyable. We hunger for success to pay it forward. Aside from the glitz and glam you see on the surface, the road to success is fraught with limited visibility, blind curves, and catastrophic hazards. The success stories we hear often sound like they happened overnight, but those stories leave out many hasty decisions, inaccurate predictions, bumbled conversations, miscalculations, and constantly shifting landscapes that successful people encounter every day.

I failed more times than I could have ever imagined when I took my first swing at adult life. And I'm not talking about small, insignificant failures, either. I'm talking about the kind of failures that haunt you—those that completely alter the landscape of your career, personal relationships, shake you to the core, and make you question all that you thought was real. I can't say I particularly enjoy failing—I'm still working on "welcoming the failure" in my own life (it's tough!)—but failure can be life's greatest teacher if you let it.

Learning the lessons of failure first requires honest introspection, which is probably the hardest part, because you have to face yourself—your entire self. The lessons of failure require you to analyze them in an objective way and dissect them enough to *make them* your educator. This step is mission critical. Have you ever wondered why we always give the best advice to our friends and loved ones, but seldom to ourselves? When we give advice to others, we depersonalize the problem, and think objectively. If you can do that for yourself, then you can extract the lesson and immediately implement it. Sure, you'll still make mistakes, but if you do it honestly, you won't make the *same* mistakes—you'll make bigger, tougher, and scarier ones. As Jim Rohn said, "Don't wish it was easier, wish you were better."

When you master this skill, failure will alchemize into a gift.

Entrepreneurs by nature are resourceful problem-solvers. Not all of us, however, are willing to examine our failures and look within. Many are quick to extract lessons when we see epic, life-changing, mind-blowing success. Yet when we fail, we try to forget about it and move on as quickly as possible. Why? Because failure is *painful*. Few people willingly tread the path of *more* resistance—it's too uncomfortable.

This is why failure is such a good instructor. When the most successful entrepreneurs encounter failure, we extract the lessons to avoid repeating them in the future. This ensures our business not only survives but prospers. When a problem surfaces (and they always do), it's Murphy's Law: "Anything that can go wrong will go wrong." Expect it. It's counterintuitive to not immediately react when issues arise. Most often we spring into action to address the problem, believing it will inch us closer to a solution. Unfortunately, that doesn't always work.

To be presumptuous, I'd say that approach is wrong.

Sometimes, you need to pause. Sometimes, not moving is the move. Sometimes, silence is the loudest thing you can say. Sometimes the problem you need to solve is not even the real problem. Pause, but don't react—*yet*. Spend time reflecting. Then, resolve, analyze, and when you're ready, respond with a well-considered solution to a well-defined problem. We should not be looking to be *right*—often there may be many right answers. Instead, we should be looking for the best solution to the real problem.

Books about how to build a billion-dollar business usually focus on aspects of the business itself—systems, management, organizational structure, and so on. That's all well and good, but the secret to success has nothing to do with that. In fact, success has little to do with the organization itself.

To me, the long-lasting, sustainable secret to success is *you*.

To build your business into an unstoppable force of nature, first, you must make *yourself* unstoppable.

With that mindset, you will grow into your greatest asset— and my deepest wish for this book is to show you what worked for me in the hopes that you can apply my lessons to your own life. In the pages that follow, I'm going to share with you my gifts from failure and what I changed in myself that eventually trickled down to all aspects of my life. I'm also going to provide guidance, actionable lessons, and essential takeaways that can translate into value.

When it comes to how to improve your business, you need to change your perspective. Instead of focusing on your business at each point of failure, I want you to start first focusing on yourself. The better you are, the better the business. In the world-famous book *7 Habits of Highly Effective People*, author Stephen Covey refers to this as a *paradigm shift*. When you commit to making this shift, you will be a more effective person. You will be in control. Over time, it'll strengthen your personal integrity, cultivate compassion, and elevate your energy. Relationships will improve because you'll show up differently, not only in meetings with important clients or colleagues but also with your family and friends. By working on yourself, you will by default improve your business, because your business is an extension of you. Think of it like this: If you are a tree's roots, trunk, and branches, and your business is the leaves, the leaves rely on a healthy tree to thrive. The same idea resonates with all other aspects of life. By creating strong roots, trunk, and branches—by creating value in yourself—you create value in your employees, your clients, and thus, your company.

Sounds easy enough, right? *Wrong*. It is simple, but not easy. As far as I'm aware, nothing you get from doing something easy is worth it unless it was pure grace. The Lord knows I'm immensely grateful for how I've been blessed on my journey. Anything worth doing is hard—raising kids, building a business, going to the gym, eating healthy consistently—but it's worth it. Trade instant gratification for long-term success.

I know this mindset through personal experience building my own private real estate business, Rastegar Property Company. We've built a strong enterprise, wholly owned at a corporate level, from basically nothing. Now, with the help of some of the greatest minds in real estate, technology, and entertainment, we're on our way to becoming a multibillion-dollar global firm. Behind every success, however, I first faced a profound failure. But every time something went wrong, instead of looking at what needed to change in my business, I looked to see what I could change in myself, because what's happening externally reflects what's happening internally. Fear, insecurity, avoidance—it all shows up in your face, your body language, and radiates outward into your life. It's important to take responsibility for *everything*.

The more I failed, the more I worked on myself. What started with a few minutes of daily meditation snowballed into a massive commitment to health and wellness. And do you know what happened? I saw more success. It positively affected my business, and as a pleasant surprise, bled into my personal life as a father and a husband, which are two of the most important roles in my life.

At times, things were uncomfortable; but learn how to be comfortable with being uncomfortable, because that's where most growth originates. They don't call them "growing pains" for nothing. Clichés are clichés for a reason. Growth and comfort cannot coexist. I despise when people say, "It's just business, it's not personal." There is nothing more personal than business, especially if it's your own.

Everything I present in the following chapters I do, and they have a direct impact on how I run my life. There is no separation between personal life and business life. Everything is intertwined. That's why whatever you do to improve yourself will naturally translate to improving your business.

I view the lessons in this book and my own process as training for life. All the "success" I've had in business directly correlates to the behaviors, habits, and goals you're about to learn. As a real estate developer, I know that if the foundation is bad, nothing else will matter. Make your foundation solid, deep, and wide. If you don't have a solid foundation, it doesn't matter how good the walls are or the interior design, you're just putting "lipstick on a pig"—a common real estate term used to describe light renovations and mediocre upgrades. Compared to what we do at Rastegar, this is the path of least resistance. We take existing properties down to the studs, re-imagine them and create value by delivering a superior product, or we simply build the asset from the ground up, the right way.

This book isn't me on a soapbox, either. I have a lot to learn and am more aware of that today than ever. Mine for the jewels, apply what works for you, and discard the rest. If a few of the lessons I have learned will help you self-develop, then they are worth sharing. Use what works for you.

READ THIS BOOK IF...

"I start early and I stay late, day after day. It took me 17 years and 114 days to become an overnight success."

—LIONEL "LEO" MESSI

This is a self-development book for entrepreneurs or anyone aspiring to reach a level of success that is unfathomable to most, in any industry. Everything in this book is a layer of personal development that will positively impact your business, regardless of your field.

This is not a book for employees seeking a promotion. It is not a book for those who want to be average, either. I don't do average or mediocre. This book is for the dreamers with extraordinary dreams. The world needs more dreamers, movers, and shakers—now more than ever. We need you to share your dreams with the world. You're reading this book because you have a calling. Listen for it and *GO*. As Steve Jobs said, "They [dreamers] push the human race forward, and while some may see them as the crazy ones, we see genius, because the ones who are crazy enough to think they can change the world, are the ones who do."

Everyone needs help in achieving larger-than-life goals. The greatest performers, entertainers, and competitors of any genre all have coaches and mentors—that's where this book comes in. Nothing great was ever accomplished alone. Success and fulfillment are team sports.

Although this book will explain relatively simple concepts to implement, they will not be easy. *Everything is hard.* The sooner you accept that, the better. Stop wasting time complaining, and use that energy for something constructive, like taking massive action.

Thomas Edison once said, "Opportunity is missed by most people because it is dressed in overalls and looks like work." In my case, opportunity showed up in lululemon workout gear. If you're relying on opportunities to come your way, you'll wait forever. Only by putting yourself out there, doing the hard work, and taking action to achieve your dreams will you increase your chances of getting *lucky*. Thomas Jefferson got it right when he said, "The harder I work, the more luck

I have." Pablo Picasso had a similar perspective: "Inspiration exists, but it has to find you working."

As you read this book, you will begin to look at your own failures and deferred dreams. You may even feel *more* like a failure. This will change once you take total responsibility for your life. You have more control than you assume. Don't be a victim. In fact, you are not a victim. Life is not happening *to* you. It has been and always will be happening *for* you. I truly believe that, and my own life is proof.

If you're not taking responsibility for yourself, this book is not for you. It's time to take responsibility for your decisions and your actions (or lack thereof)—past, present, and future. If you don't, then you are not in control, and your business will reflect that. If you're not in control, that means something else is, whether that's other people or a detrimental state of mind. Do not be a pawn in someone else's game, including your own self-doubts (the worst enemy of all).

If you feel like a pawn right now, don't fret—remember that a pawn can take down a king.

MY STORY, THUS FAR

"No man ever achieved worth-while success who did not, at one time or other, find himself with at least one foot hanging well over the brink of failure."

—NAPOLEON HILL

I come from a paternal bloodline of highly educated and respected individuals who originate from a province of Iran called Taleghan. My mother's family is German, although she was born in Hawaii. Pretty much everyone on my father's side of the family has a master's or a PhD and either work as lawyers, doctors, or scientists. My grandfather, Dr. Hossein Rastegar, and my attorney father, Sheida Rastegar, were my childhood heroes. My grandfather not only worked as a medical doctor and psychiatrist, but he was also an incredible athlete. He competed in the Iranian National Games in cycling and several other track and field events, where he won seven gold medals. He was a true renaissance man.

Then came the 1979 Iranian Revolution, which changed everything overnight. My uncles, my aunt, and my father were studying in Austin, Texas, at the time, so they immediately lost their visas and had to start over. I'm not sure anyone recovers from that trauma. My family was close to the Shah (*King* in Farsi), and since we were not Muslim, my grandparents had to flee to Turkey to seek asylum. Through the grace of God, a donkey, and frostbite, they survived. My family eventually reunited in Austin, but they lost their possessions in the process, including their homes, land, bank accounts, and priceless heirlooms. Fortunately, they never lost their mindset, culture, or family values. The Rastegar Creed, as my father says, is "Courage." This is the plight of many Iranian Americans who experienced this heartbreak but then found safety, love, and prosperity in our great country. My heart goes out to them and to all who share a similar story.

Growing up in a family that valued education above all, I initially wanted to be a doctor like my grandfather, but he inspired me to be a businessman. We'd walk the streets of Austin and Dallas, and he would point at skyscrapers and tell me to "buy all of them one day." He once said, "I want you to be wealthy. America is the best place in the world right now to create massive wealth, which you can then use to help others." He believed real estate was the best opportunity, and he wanted me to be successful enough so that one day I could buy back the land in Iran that my family had lost—which I fully intend on doing.

When I was growing up, my family didn't have the money to go on many trips, so I spent a lot of time reading. My dad always said I couldn't stop reading even if I tried. Throughout this book, I pay homage to the great thinkers, philosophers, and authors by extracting key takeaways from their wisdom, so you can benefit without spending the time or money reading the originals. For the bookworms out there, you'll find my "further reading" list of recommended books in the appendix.

Despite my family's seemingly endless brainpower, I wasn't particularly gifted or special in any way. I was blessed to be born in the United States, especially in Austin. But otherwise, I faced a lot of adversity growing up. My parents divorced when I was two years old—young enough not to understand, but old enough to remember. Due to the trauma from the divorce, I developed a severe speech impediment that I spent seven brutal years correcting. Hours turned to days of reading in front of the mirror, trying desperately to enunciate words properly. I had an awful lisp (and I'm still wondering which cruel person put an "S" in the word *lisp*). To make matters worse, growing up I was neither a stellar student nor a star athlete.

My *Baba* (father in Farsi) taught me something priceless,

however. He taught me how to think for myself and to listen to my inner voice. Despite the struggles of feeling less than average, I first started setting goals for myself in high school; one of my earliest was to become an "ultra-successful, high achiever" (whatever that meant!). All I knew is that I yearned to be better—it was a *must*. I had no idea how I was going to get there at the age of sixteen, but I kept it top of mind.

By the time I was ready for college, I found myself extraordinarily unprepared, and ended up attending two different community colleges. Ultimately, I transferred to Texas A&M University, graduating with honors and earning an English degree. Even though I went to law school, I was rejected from all the schools I applied to but one: St. Mary's University School of Law in San Antonio, Texas. I felt like a failure being rejected from many of the schools I wanted to attend, but that failure led to the *right* school for me. It was a blessing to attend such a prestigious school, which opened the door for me to start (the first iteration of) my real estate company by using a $3,000 loan and the remainder of my scholarship money. So, when I say I built my business from modest means and grit, I mean it. And if I did it, you can do it better.

For me, one thing was for certain: I was determined to make my life matter for others by helping solve problems that move the world forward. To be successful, I needed to build myself into the highest skyscraper—but the taller the building, the deeper you must dig to build the foundation. That is physics. So deep I went, and the deeper I dug, the higher my skyscraper grew. The deeper you go, the harder it is. Be ready.

After a few stepping-stones early in my career on Wall Street,

I launched Rastegar in 2015. We've successfully participated in projects in thirty-eight cities, twelve states, and seven different asset classes, including apartments, self-storage, master plan communities, retail, and office. Our collective team of more than a hundred people operates either internally or as consultants and contractors. I'm proud to say that we are a private company that never sold ownership at the corporate level. This affords us the privilege to roll out a revolutionary proprietary profit-sharing program for our loyal staff.

I believe the main reason our company experienced healthy, sustainable success is that I focused on fixing myself first and sharing my failures and the lessons with our entire team. I did this without shame and without sugarcoating. We are not after perfection; we seek excellence.

That should be your focus, too, and you certainly don't have to do it alone. In fact, it is not possible. *I stand on the shoulders of giants.* I credit a lot of my growth and success to the hundreds of people I've had the great honor to learn from throughout my life, whether through mentorship, books (mostly books), seminars, conferences, YouTube clips, podcasts, policymakers, and life coaches.

Without a doubt, my most important teachers were the many failures I've encountered along the way—one of which still haunts me to this day (more on that later). At the time, it was my failure of all failures. In hindsight, however, it was an inflection point that pushed me to continuously learn, evolve, and grow. The marathon continues.

This book is broken down into three parts. In Part 1, we'll

dig deep into your mental wellbeing. To build a skyscraper, you need a solid, deep foundation. In Part 2, we'll focus on the external, looking out and up as we start to physically build upon that foundation. Finally, in Part 3, we'll look beyond the physical skyscraper you've built and focus on the transcendental.

Each chapter centers around a personal failure of mine, how I overcame it by focusing on myself, and how the results then transformed not only me as a person, but everything I touched, whether that was my business, my family life, or my personal relationships. Learn from my failures, apply the lessons to your own life, and reap the benefits. Stop worrying about your business as a *business* and start focusing on yourself. When you focus on yourself, you too can transform lead into gold, like the great alchemists of the past. It's in your hands.

If a traumatized, below-average child of divorced immigrant parents with a severe speech impediment could do it, so can you. I expect you to surpass all my achievements. That's my greatest hope and the reason I wrote this for you.

YOU HAVE GREATNESS WITHIN YOU

Steve Jobs loved to point out that the things we value today—like the smartphone in your pocket—were created by regular people just like you and me. These creators weren't more talented than us. They weren't more intelligent. They were simply tapping into their greatness and had the courage to put their ideas out into the world.

But as Les Brown once said, "You cannot expect to achieve

new goals or move beyond your present circumstances unless you change." So, if you're ready to break through barriers, to quit limiting yourself, to unlearn bad mental data, and to achieve your wildest entrepreneurial dreams, then you've picked up the right book.

You have greatness within you. You might not believe that, yet. You might doubt yourself due to experiences that might have "proven" otherwise, but I assure you, it is there.

We'll start with how the biggest failure of my life turned into one of my most precious gifts.

CHAPTER 1

TOO GOOD TO BE TRUE

"Success is most often achieved by those who don't know that failure is inevitable."

—COCO CHANEL

I got my first taste of working in law as a young teenager.

John Hampton Read II is one of my dad's dearest friends and a famous attorney whom I worked for as a thirteen-year-old. I performed an epic amount of legal grunt work, but most of the time I was taking out the garbage, opening mail, and carrying his briefcase. He also let me borrow his classic Corvette from time to time against my father's advice, so at least there was that.

After I finished law school in 2008, I started working as an attorney for my uncle, doing whatever I could to add value to his law firm. Unexpectedly, two clients walked into our office and changed the entire trajectory of my career. Just like that, fate reared its head, and in 2009, I inadvertently found myself launching a global entertainment company.

Now mind you, I knew nothing about the entertainment industry. I also didn't have any experience launching a business—let alone running one. But as it goes with such ventures, failures occurred, experience was gained, and lessons were learned.

The biggest lesson I learned early in my career is that launching a business has less to do with the business, and way more with who you are as a person.

In February 2010, my wrestling coach from middle school, Michael Gloria Chiarelli (whom I knew simply as "Coach"), was in Dallas with his childhood friend, Anthony Orso, who is one of the top real estate finance people on the planet. They happened to be in town for a Dallas Cowboys game and were hosting a dinner for some of the executives and a few star players. I grew up with Michael's godson, Joey Marzuola, who remains one of my best friends almost thirty years later. Coach came from a wealthy New York family. His father was a famous Venetian plaster painter whose clients included celebrities, political figures, and billionaires.

Since they were in Dallas, and Coach knew I was obsessed with real estate, he wanted to introduce me to Anthony—but it was going to be a tough introduction. Anthony was the managing director at Credit Suisse and responsible for over $400 billion in global real estate lending. Coach initially invited another childhood friend of mine, Major Miller, to dinner, but when he reminded Coach I was in town, the seats were all filled. Major then graciously gave me his seat at the table, which I gladly accepted. I later learned I was the only person Coach ever introduced to Anthony for business purposes, despite hundreds, if not thousands, of other requests. As they say, Coach vouched for me, from one Italian to another.

Over dinner, Coach urged me to tell Anthony the story about how I helped an event promoter avoid litigation with a local nightclub for backing out of a deal to host an NBA All-Star party for LeBron James and Drake (who may be a superstar now, but few had heard of him at the time). Instead of suing, I suggested they let me help them move their event to another location. After calling my various contacts in Dallas, I found them another suitable venue. I even helped them restructure their pricing plan and made sure everything was good to go from a legal standpoint.

"Wow, Ari." Coach laughed. "Nicely done. You've always been a go-getter"—this, coming from a guy who was always light on compliments, unless unequivocally merited.

Going over the details of my story with Anthony was how we bonded. Impressed with what he heard, he came up with an idea on the spot. "What if we started a global entertainment company?" he asked. While the real estate industry was still slowly recovering from the Great Recession, Anthony was interested in exploring other ways to make money. Luckily, the 2011 Super Bowl was scheduled to take place in Dallas the following year; what better way to entertain his affluent clients than inviting them to lavish parties organized by his own company?

He was willing to take a chance on me, and that was all I ever prayed for. Naturally, I jumped at the opportunity to align myself with him. I still think a critical reason he took a chance on me was because of his eldest son, Stephen Orso, who wanted to work on this as much as I did. Working with Anthony was a solid opportunity to progress toward my high school goal of becoming a high achiever. I looked up to him, and I still do. I soon discovered, proximity to your heroes is magic. Proximity has power.

By the time we finished dinner, Capital A Entertainment was born—*he* was the Capital, and I was the *A*. My only condition was that I brought two of my childhood friends, Major Miller and Luis Ortiz, to come help. He agreed. So, we moved to Manhattan.

Our team set our eyes on throwing two parties the week of Super Bowl XLV in February 2011—one on Friday and one on Saturday—which gave us a little less than a year to organize. We dove right in. As a brand-new company with no track record, in an industry that functions on connections and knowing the right people, we had our work cut out for us. And wow, did we have a lot to do—a daunting, inconceivable amount. We had to find venues, figure out how to sign top-tier talent, engage corporate sponsors, and market the events to sell tables and individual tickets.

It was an unnerving insane amount to process, but we were eager to accomplish the unthinkable, and somehow, we knew we could do it. To say the small staff of five at Capital A worked *hard* would be a severe understatement. There isn't a word to describe how tirelessly we worked. Our intensity bordered on absolute insanity. The timelines were unreasonable. The team and I made hundreds of calls per day. We traveled back and forth from one coast to the other to meet with the biggest celebrities and brands in the world—sometimes just for one meeting only to hop on a return flight the same day. We didn't have any fancy office equipment, nor did any of us have any formal experience, but we did have a unified goal and the will to succeed. Like Bill Gates—who famously claimed he didn't take a single day off in his twenties—there was no such thing as a day off for us. Every day was a Monday. Hell, there wasn't even time to sleep, and when we did, we did it at our desks. It was nonstop, all day, every day for more than a year.

We got thousands of no's, but we remained relentless. There's a proverb that states, "The sale doesn't start until they say 'No.' Otherwise, it's just a request or a question, not a sale." It was the most magical yet vulnerable time of my life. In a matter of months, I went from living on Major's couch after law school to meeting with the CEO of Sports Illustrated, the Black-Eyed Peas, and P. Diddy—just to name a few.

We were up against some thirty other companies that had been throwing parties for decades—giants like Maxim, the juggernaut of Super Bowl parties (which we tried to buy, but that's a story for another book). We didn't just hold our own; we did something special and competed at the highest level.

Through grit and luck, countless cold calls, and no sleep, which I don't recommend, especially after reading Arianna Huffington's book *The Sleep Revolution*, we signed the Black-Eyed Peas to perform during our Friday night party (they were also the Super Bowl halftime headliner that year). David Guetta and Diplo would open for the Peas. (In 2011, Guetta was voted as number one in *DJ Magazine's* Top 100 poll.) For our Saturday event, P. Diddy headlined, and Clinton Sparks with DJ Irie was on the turntables. Our corporate sponsors included Nivea for Men, Facebook (now Meta), Sports Illustrated, and Tequila Avión (yes, the tequila brand that was a major plotline in the seventh season of HBO's show *Entourage*).

Leading up to Super Bowl XLV, everything *seemed* wildly successful. Most tables were purchased for $50,000 apiece, and we sold thousands of tickets. Capital A came out of nowhere and aligned with the biggest acts and brands in the world within a year of forming the LLC—on a shoestring budget, no less. Maxim usually gets the A-list celebrities and the biggest names, but we came out on top that year. Even Mark Zuckerberg showed up to our party. Luck is a powerful thing—especially when it finds you working.

While preparing for the Super Bowl parties, we were also planning our third event for the NBA All-Star weekend, which took place the following week in Los Angeles. Within a year of forming Capital A, we organized two back-to-back weekend parties.

The most established brands in the world throw one party a year. We did three.

Committed to creating the best experience possible, we managed to rent the Playboy Mansion and contracted Snoop Dogg, Blake Griffin, Kevin Love, Fabolous, and Trey Songz.

It was a surreal feeling to walk through the Playboy Mansion in preparation of the party (mind you, this was well before the horrors of the Playboy brand were revealed). I could see the event in my head, could envision playing poker with Hef, a dream come true. MySpace was scheduled to livestream, which was a big deal at the time since it would be the first time any platform streamed an event of this magnitude. We were later told that over a hundred million people tuned in (not sure the number was accurate, but it felt good to hear) because the concept was so revolutionary.

Working on these three events simultaneously with no time to spare often felt like a losing battle, but we did it. Through providence and hundreds of tiny miracles in a wildly slippery, cut-throat industry, all the pieces came together.

Although it was hectic, stressful, and at times chaotic, we were poised to profit over $5 million from the Super Bowl weekend and another $2 million from the Playboy Mansion. We somehow pulled off the inconceivable—and I was elated. I got a glimpse of the good life. *I'm in my twenties, and I'm poised to be a multimillionaire*, I thought to myself giddily. The idea was unfathomable just months before.

And then, failure reared its ugly head.

FREAK ICE STORM

On the Tuesday leading up to the Super Bowl, Dallas was hit with a totally unexpected and catastrophic ice storm, the biggest in the history of Texas at the time. It was absurd—a crippling ice storm in Texas? You have got to be kidding me!

Is God telling me something? I thought to myself.

The freak winter storm coated the city with ice—together, with much of the east coast, including New York City, down to Richmond and Atlanta, but Dallas was the worst. Temperatures plunged into the teens, paralyzing Dallas–Fort Worth International Airport and canceling flights—including my own. Since I couldn't fly directly to Dallas from New York City, I rented a car and drove to Richmond, Virginia, in the ice storm, eight hours straight, starting at midnight from Manhattan. I then flew to Atlanta and traded my ticket with a retired couple to board the last flight to Dallas before all the airports shut down. The storm continued throughout the week, dumping several inches of ice and snow in an area not equipped to deal with it. Something as simple as having snowplows was "not necessary" in Dallas at the time. Hundreds of flights were canceled, many of them on Friday, the night of our first party.

With no way for many of our guests to travel to the city, they started filing chargebacks for their table and ticket purchases. A few returned dollars then turned into thousands. Then millions. While I went to sleep a millionaire, I woke up broke. It was an absolute bloodbath.

I panicked. *What on earth am I going to do?* (I feel nauseated again while writing these words.)

Somehow, I still felt that we could pull it off. I was determined to make it a success. The Super Bowl was going to happen, rain or shine—or in our case, a freak ice storm—so we decided not to cancel. *The show must go on.* Maybe the deep confidence and faith I had was from shock and paralyzing fear, but my belief that our parties would succeed moved me from panic to peace.

Okay, peace is a stretch, but we did put our heads down and prayed a little, and then we got after it.

And the show did go on—without a hitch. All of our acts showed up, which was obviously a huge relief. In addition, three hundred celebrities walked the red carpet, including Cameron Diaz, Alex Rodriguez, and Hugh Jackman—celebrities I dreamed of meeting my whole life. But because it wasn't what I envisioned, I couldn't enjoy myself. I was halfheartedly smiling. My head wasn't in the right place. In the back of my mind, all I kept hearing was what a complete failure this was—what a complete failure *I was*. What would Anthony think? What would he say? At one point, I searched for a tranquilizer because I felt like I was going to have a full-on panic attack. (I didn't find any). The anxiety was physical and debilitating. With my disappointment following me like a dark cloud over my head, I was left to run on adrenaline, knowing this was going to work or I was going to die trying.

Clearly, the two-day event was a huge failure from a profitability standpoint. We should have planned and budgeted a lot better than we did. That said, it ended up being the most magical, unbelievable experience for those who attended, not only because of the lineup, but also because there just weren't as many people, which created a more intimate setting.

Even so, I didn't have the words to express how angry I was at the time. In fact, I still feel hurt, sad, mad, and a myriad of other emotions just thinking about it.

> I set myself up for failure because I was committed to perfection and left no room for external factors that could alter the outcomes. Never again. *Failure*.

HIDING UNDER THE COVERS FOREVER

"Everyone has a plan until they get punched in the face."

—MIKE TYSON

Despite the fun our guests had, I woke up on Sunday morning wanting to die. It was one of the worst mornings of my life. I didn't even go to the Super Bowl. I just laid in bed, paralyzed with fear, drowning in misery. Was I insanely hard on myself? Yes. Did I realize this and stop my victim mentality? No.

I can't go on like this, I thought to myself, curled up in the fetal position on the bed in my hotel room while Major, Luis, and Joey tried to cheer me up. *I put in ten years of work in one year. If that doesn't cut it, I don't know what will.*

I was done, mentally. Floored.

I couldn't fathom being blessed with more miracles happening for us as they did that year. I couldn't fathom working any harder. Self-doubt crept in, and I found myself asking if success was really something I could achieve. I was ready to quit. Thoughts of moving to Costa Rica danced around my head. *Maybe I can make a living as a writer? I'll work on the beach and bartend at night to help pay the bills. I have a law degree, maybe I can open a little practice and help people with immigration law once a week. I'll live in flip-flops and enjoy my youth. Fuck working as hard as I did this past year if it's all going to just blow up in my face at the last minute, I'm done.*

Ring, ring, ring.

I pulled the sheets from over my head to see who was calling. It was Anthony. *Crap.* This whole venture was a failure, and the guy who believed in me and funded the whole thing was calling. I was petrified. I lost the money. All I felt was pure anguish and embarrassment. Not many things feel worse than letting a mentor down, and I felt like such an idiot. I really wanted it to work. I wanted to make him proud. I was so confident that our plans were going to work. *How* did this happen? I questioned God and the universe; the fabric of my existence was unraveling.

The first thing he said was, "Hey, come to my room."

Oh God. My stomach dropped to my ankles. I wasn't ready to face him, but I knew I had to. I walked down the hallway to his room in absolute agony.

"Ready to go to LA?" he casually asked once I entered his room, where he was pacing as he packed.

"Are you out of your mind?" I responded. "I can't go to LA. I want to jump off the top of this hotel."

"Huh? Shake it off." He said it so nonchalantly. So effortlessly. I was in shock. I was expecting a shank to the chest, which I would have gladly accepted.

After talking for a bit longer, I went from feeling the lowest of the low to feeling like I could redeem myself. He was right. There was no time to sulk. I had to focus on our party at the Playboy Mansion. I needed to get it together. Although we wouldn't recover the funds lost in Dallas to be profitable, we at least had a shot to break even in the City of Angels.

I didn't have the energy or experience to examine this failure. But Anthony's confidence and composure taught me something that words cannot do justice. It took years of introspection before I learned the gift: fail forward and keep moving.

CITY OF ANGELS, HERE WE COME

The day after the Super Bowl, the Capital A team got on a plane and flew to LA to get ready for Friday night. We rented a hostel in Venice Beach on Rose Street to house the team while we prepared for the event. (Fast forward, I got married on the beach in front of that same hostel). On Wednesday, we did a walkthrough of the Mansion, and everything was lining up nicely.

This will be a night to remember, I thought to myself. *Redemption.*

In 2011, before Hugh Hefner's passing and the property was sold, the Playboy Mansion was the crème de la crème; you simply could not find a more iconic venue in California. At the time, Mr. Hefner had thoroughly established a reputation for hosting legendary parties with exclusive guests. And here we were, premiering our first West Coast party there. It was breathtaking.

That evening, eating dinner in our rental, watching the news, a reporter made an alarming announcement:

> Breaking news: Bacteria that cause Legionnaire's disease was found at the Playboy Mansion. Los Angeles County Health Department officials have shut down the Playboy Mansion indefinitely.

You've got to be kidding me!

We dropped everything and immediately scrambled to find a new place. We had forty-eight hours, and I wasn't familiar with LA. Here I was frantic yet—again. I was zero for two at this point and barely hanging on. Someone told me to check out Voyeur, an old strip club in West Hollywood that was converted into a super high-end lounge, the hardest door in LA.

Amid all the chaos, there was fate. As we walked through Voyeur, Luis noticed a lovely lady leaning against the bar and suggested I go talk to her. The last thing on my mind was socializing, but something possessed me to take the plunge. I was a bachelor, so why not? Anything to change my mindset, even for a moment. I gently approached her and respectfully introduced myself. "Hi, I'm Ari. Uh, my friend," I pointed to Luis over the crowd, "nudged me to come say hi. Sorry if I'm bothering you."

A *long* bit of silence.

"Hi. I'm Kellie."

"Nice to meet you." I offered to buy her a drink, but she said no (we ended up having tequila shots later).

"So, what are you doing here?"

"I'm here with my boss." She pointed to a man behind her.

"That is *Johnny Depp*. Uh, what do you do?" I was playing it cool, but Johnny was my Hollywood hero. I even had his poster on my wall as a kid, embarrassingly enough.

"I'm a corporate flight attendant, and I do some personal assistant work for him. What are you doing here?" I told her about the pickle we were in, including the prior weekend's fiasco during the Super Bowl.

"You threw the Super Bowl Party with P. Diddy and the Sports Illustrated party with the Peas?" Kellie asked. "I was there! It was one of the best parties I've ever been to in my life!" We exchanged numbers and planned to see each other again.

Serendipity. Or as Matthew McConaughey would say, "Greenlight."

Back to business.

The next morning, we frantically contacted potential venues. Luckily, we secured the Conga Room, located at LA Live, an entertainment complex downtown. Tickets for the Playboy Mansion had sold for thousands of dollars, because the Mansion itself is a huge draw. Unfortunately, we couldn't charge anywhere near that amount for the Conga Room. We went from $2,000 a ticket to $75. We expected roughly one thousand people at the Mansion. We went from projecting millions of dollars in revenue to thousands of dollars. *Failure.*

I was beyond devastated. All the sleepless nights, the endless hours, the stress, the constant calling, pitching, and selling—everything we'd worked our asses off for ended up fully crashing and burning. My dream of making an incredible living disappeared as easily as blowing out a candle. I'd encountered failure before, but this one was full-on soul-crushing.

Despite my utter devastation, once again, the show had to go on. And it did. Fabolous, Trey Songz, and Nate Dogg performed (we were later told it was Nate Dogg's last performance before he died. Rest in peace, King). Blake Griffin, a rookie that year and now an NBA superstar, was one of the hosts too. He was a bit shy at the time, so I introduced him to some of the bigger-named guests. Even Kellie showed up!

Despite our financial loss, the party was one for the books. The attendees showered us with compliments, but that didn't make up for my feeling of complete and utter failure.

No one could have ever predicted the weather in Dallas or the airborne bacteria breakout in Los Angeles, but I still viewed them as personal failures. I've always taken full responsibility for everything that happens in my life. So should you. Needless to say, I took this very hard.

History teaches us that entrepreneurs have a *dip* or a low point in their journey. My journey contained two low points, and the second one was that final nail in the coffin. After working all year with inhumane dedication and alien work ethic, in the end, it was a financial loss. There was no way to recover from that. Those catastrophes were the bottom for me. Rock bottom.

I intended to be a hero. Instead, I felt like a zero. Even though the weather was no one's fault, we could have planned better. Today, I understand that even if something is not your fault, it *is* your problem. The party in LA was supposed to be my redemption, pulling things together, persevering, and winning in the end. Nope!

It was the end of Capital A, and the beginning of my new life. Soon, I would learn that a disaster in your current career often marks the beginning of your next career. If you're forced off the track, then find another track.

There are countless clichés to describe this moment, but in the end, the end of Capital A was a blessing because it forced me to revisit my dream of real estate. By early 2011, the markets had begun to recover. I saw my opening—and took it.

CONNECTING THE DOTS BACKWARDS

"You can't connect the dots looking forward; you can only connect them looking backwards. So you have to trust that the dots will somehow connect in your future. You have to trust in something— your gut, destiny, life, karma, whatever. This approach has never let me down, and it has made all the difference in my life."

—STEVE JOBS

Capital A still haunts me, and I have nightmares about it to this day. I often joke about how I'm still tired and haven't caught up on all the sleep I lost that year.

I've always been a man of God and a big believer in destiny, and the gifts I've been given were granted to do great things for others. I can now look back at these "failures" and realize that although I might not have reached my intended outcome, plenty of lessons were learned, and several other positive outcomes were manifested.

As the old Yiddish proverb says, "Man plans, God laughs." Capital A was a gift. The lessons from the experience I carry with me to this day. I now stress test for any conceivable problem that could arise and constantly create contingency strategies. I don't expect perfection; I prepare to adapt.

Failing at that profound level was one of the greatest things that ever happened to me. It opened many doors of unexpected opportunity that I never knew existed. I developed deep relationships with people who became early clients in our real estate business. The knowledge of the entertainment industry helped us create a culture of hyper-communication and celebrity-level customer service. These are two of our foundational core values that make up part of our corporate culture. Nowadays, our customers are *celebrities* to us, which to be fair, many of them are. We honor them. Many have become some of my best friends, part of the Rastegar family.

Connecting the dots backwards, the best thing to come out of the whole experience was meeting my wife, the mother of our three magnificent children. That would never have happened if the Playboy Mansion wasn't shut down.

"Thank God you weren't successful with Capital A," Kellie now says with a chuckle and a subtle eye-roll. "You would have been a party promoter for the rest of your life instead of fulfilling your true calling." She's right. This was not my calling. Not my destiny.

By returning to real estate, I was (finally) on the *right* path. *My* path. Little did I know, I was about to learn another brutal lesson: running a business has nothing to do with business, and everything to do with *you*.

PART 1

LOOKING WITHIN: ESTABLISHING A SOLID FOUNDATION

"A successful man is one who can lay a firm foundation with the bricks that others have thrown at him."
—DAVID BRINKLEY

CHAPTER 2

BUSINESS HAS NOTHING TO DO WITH BUSINESS

"Eighty to 90 percent of success in a company has nothing to do with business at all—it's all personal."

—CAROL ROTH

Do you think we successfully signed the Black-Eyed Peas, LeBron James, P. Diddy, David Guetta, Diplo, Trey Songz, Fabolous, Snoop Dogg, Nate Dogg, and Drake because we were a well-established company? No. They worked with us because they felt something in their gut. They liked me, they liked us, they trusted us, and they believed we could achieve what we envisioned—none of which are elements of running a business, per se.

It's a truth of life: people do business with those they like. Period.

It's still painful to think about what happened with Capital A, but it was a great lesson in that running a business has less to do with systems and processes and more with who you are as a person. I learned to just ask, whereas others didn't ask because they feared rejection. Don't fear rejection. Expect it and keep asking anyway. Nothing wants to stand in front of someone who is relentless.

I learned that putting yourself out there, being transparent, and proving that you follow through on your promises took me further than a compelling mission statement or an impressive business plan. As Reid Hoffman says, "An entrepreneur is someone who will jump off a cliff and assemble an airplane on the way down." I get it, but these days I pack a parachute or two.

When working with me, one thing is certain: I will do my best to take care of your needs as if they were my own. We seek to under promise and over deliver.

Ari in Hebrew means *lion*, and I behave like a protective lion when it comes to the people I work with, whether they're family, customers, or anyone in my pride. When I was flying across the country to meet with managers and CEOs, they could *feel* that in me, which is why they took the leap of faith to align. I'm not bragging. It's a fact. They told me themselves.

I could see my hard work beginning to pay off. The person I yearned to be, my authentic self, the person I was working to become, the person I chiseled out of marble, had begun to emerge. I now exuded passion and conviction—intangible characteristics that are more important in business than explaining numbers on a spreadsheet. Of course, you always present the financials and do the math. I'm a data, research, and numbers freak. At Rastegar, we run numerous worst-case scenarios before making business decisions, without using wishful thinking. We let the best answer prevail based on math married to the human element. Especially after Capital A, I check and double-check what could go wrong, to manage the potential risks. No one has a crystal ball, me especially. All I can do is try to make the best decisions with the available data. Nothing is guaranteed, so plan accordingly. Quite literally, everything has risk. We manage risk for a living. I vowed early in my career to work ruthlessly to either die or make it work—and that's where grit comes in.

The Greek philosopher Socrates is credited with saying, "The one thing that I know is that I know nothing." What he meant by that is the more you know, the more you know you don't know—and that certainly summed up my journey until this point. In the same vein, Donald Rumsfeld said, "There are things we don't know. But there are also unknown unknowns. There are things we don't know we don't know." That's how I operate now, humble to the universe of possibilities, both good and bad.

Now I spend more time analyzing how we could lose and planning around those scenarios to reduce risk. By focusing on not losing, we believe that the probability of succeeding increases. This strategy is at the heart of what we do.

My life took a drastic turn after Capital A, and I felt in shambles. I had worked myself to near death. We set unreal goals and met most of them, despite both events ending in financial disaster. After shutting down Capital A, I returned to real estate. Over the following couple of years, I worked for a few prominent real estate developers in New York City, gaining priceless experience in the field.

At the same time, I was also in the early years of building a marriage, which had its own challenges. Kellie and I got married seven months after we met. I went from thinking I would be a bachelor forever to being a husband. The transition took some adjusting. To top everything off, three months into our marriage, we were expecting our first child, Victoria, which only added to the pressure of trying to figure out the right path for me and our growing family.

Despite the things that went well for me, I still had a lot to learn.

I mean, *a lot*. Much more than I thought. I didn't even know what I didn't know.

It was all overwhelming, and I felt lost.

> The failure to get my mindset right was devastating. Mental health and confidence took a backseat as I tried to figure out my career path.

I was working for other people, which was fine, but I still felt this deep divine calling that I was meant to do something better, something meaningful. I knew I wouldn't reach my goal of becoming ultra-successful working for someone else. The entrepreneurial spirit within me was itching to get out, but I didn't feel ready. I lacked confidence. I needed help.

I'd been an avid student of personal development since middle school. I applied the many, many lessons I learned from giants like Napoleon Hill, Tony Robbins, and Dale Carnegie, but for the first time, I had to look inward. I looked at myself in the mirror one day and said, "Dude, something is off, and the only variable is you." That hurt.

I didn't know where to start though. As Pablo Picasso would say, "You can't see the picture when you're in the frame." Tony talks about when people change, it's either from one of two things: inspiration or desperation. This was a desperate time for me.

GRIT JUXTAPOSED WITH HARD WORK

"We like to think of our champions and idols as superheroes who were born different from us. We don't like to think of them as relatively ordinary people who made themselves extraordinary."

—CAROL DWECK

As desperate as I was, I also believed in myself. To achieve greatness, to rise to the next challenge, I was ready to work to get myself back on track.

And by work, I mean relentless, unstoppable, borderline manic, *hard* work.

Elon Musk's perspective stuck with me: "Nobody ever changed the world on forty hours a week." I work 120 hours a week, so in ten years, I have done three times what the average person has, which really amounts to five times because of compounded growth.

That's significant. How would all that experience and knowledge contribute to achieving your dreams?

Working 120 hours a week obviously comes at a cost. You will have to make sacrifices. That's just the reality if you want to reach out-of-this-world goals. Time will be taken away from other things, whether that's family, traveling, or hobbies. You don't get to do it all; there's no such thing as work-life balance. You must pick your battles. For everything that you do, there's a decision you're making to not do something else. It sucks, and it's hard, especially if you have a family and want to have a social life. The way I see it, I'm making a long-term investment in *their* future, so the investment now will be worth it in the long run for those I love. I've always thought long-term, even as a child. Another gift.

At one point, Will Smith was *the* person in Hollywood, and the highest-paid actor in the world. When someone asked him how he did it, his response resonated with me deeply: "I will not be outworked, period. You might have more talent than me. You might be smarter than me. You might be sexier than me. You might be all those things. But if we get on a treadmill together, there are two things: You're getting off first, or I'm going to die. It's really that simple." That I understood. He was talking about grit.

Grit is defined as "a positive, noncognitive trait based on an individual's perseverance of effort combined with the passion for a particular long-term goal or end state." When working to achieve out-of-this world goals, it takes a lot of grit to persevere.

What I didn't understand at the time, however, is that grit

is not enough. With Capital A, I put in the work. I had grit. But I was heading in the wrong direction. I had the wrong map. If you aren't pursuing your *authentic* calling—whether you're not passionate about what you do or suspect you're in the wrong business—it's not going to work. At least not to the level it could if you are living congruently with your natural gifts. You have them—we all have them—but you must find them.

Pulling all-nighters, dependent on obscene amounts of caffeine to stay awake, is not a healthy way of life. It's also not sustainable. To be successful, you must have sustainability, scalability, and growth. These are typically business terms, but they absolutely apply to you as an individual. It's important to note now that you cannot work excessively at the expense of your health.

I know this now. My focus wasn't on taking care of myself. Luckily, the universe intervened and offered me a chance to change my perspective.

LIFE COACH

"It ain't what you don't know that gets you into trouble. It's what you know for sure that just ain't so."

—MARK TWAIN

In 2011, the concept of "life coaches" was relatively new. I came across The Handel Method, an executive coaching methodology founded by Lauren Handel Zander and Beth Handel. They revolutionized the concept of self-improvement by focusing on radical personal accountability and diving deep into the patterns and personal history that hold us back. Lauren's TEDx talk, titled "No One is Coming to Save You: Becoming Your Own Hero," struck a chord with me (you should watch it too!), and I fell in love with her teachings, including her book *Maybe It's You*.

She also scared me. It was a visceral experience. I had a lot to learn about myself. It was time to look in the mirror. I did not like what I saw. I could do better. Much better.

The Handel Method has been taught at schools and universities, and their private clients included professors, politicians, award-winning artists, Fortune 500 CEOs, and celebrities, including Hugh Jackman, who has been very outspoken about his dramatic transformation.

I took a chance and called, certain that I needed the Handel Method in my life. I wanted Lauren. Her assistant made it clear that she "curates who she talks to and only takes on a handful of clients," but I somehow managed to set up a quick call for Lauren to vet me. After speaking with her, she agreed to meet me in person for a more in-depth interview. But before that, I had to complete an extensive questionnaire that tackled all sorts of topics, such as my history, goals, dreams, career, money management, sex, romance, and family. It asked questions I'd never thought about before—like why I hadn't reached my goals and dreams. If you want the right answer, you must ask the right question. It was exhaustive and intense, but I took it very seriously. It took me roughly twenty-three hours to finish.

First impressions matter, so I wore a gray suit and arrived

early to our meeting in New York City. Lauren didn't waste any time with pleasantries and instead dove straight into business, tearing my completed homework apart. In real estate, when we look at old properties, we have to assess whether they are worth fixing or if it would be better to just tear it all down and build from scratch. Listening to Lauren and experiencing my personal emotional dissection (with a scalpel!) within moments of meeting, I quickly understood that I was a tear-down. We had to start from scratch.

"You know what your problem is?" she asked. "You suffer from a victim mentality that you cultivated." She also pointed out a negative inner dialogue of how I spoke to myself.

> I started to connect the dots. This is why the failures of Capital A were so hard on me. I internalized external factors, and somehow the negative inner voice in my head convinced me that it was all my responsibility.

She was spot on. I beat myself up when things went wrong and took responsibility for things that weren't my fault or in my control. She called it my "God Stick" that I beat myself with to the point of detriment.

My inner dialogue was brutal and often rendered me unproductive and anxious.

I was the one holding myself back.

I went into the meeting expecting to find out what to do with my life and how to reach my goal of ultra-success. Instead,

I walked out the door with an entirely new realization: *Oh God! I have to get me right. I have so much work to do on myself.*

And that was a colossal understatement.

PEELING AN ONION

To achieve the things I wanted, I needed to be brutally, ridiculously honest about *everything*—the good and especially the bad. Lauren was only interested in the truth—which I found perplexing at first. She'd ask, "Are you telling yourself a bunch of lies?" We're all guilty of this. I had to hold a mirror up to myself and acknowledge my flaws and start fixing them, now. No one teaches us to befriend the demons we have inside, or how to manage them. We simply are unaware of the damage they inflict—I know I sure wasn't.

Nowadays I know my demons by their first names. We are begrudging friends. I know their tricks and tactics to pull me out of my higher self. Now, I talk back and act accordingly. But it took me a while to get there.

Working on myself was like peeling an onion. I would tackle one area at a time, carving out my internal garbage. As I slowly evolved into a different person with each iteration, I discovered another layer that needed fixing. Within that first year, I went through five or six evolutions of reinventing myself. Each role in my life required different strategies to address different responsibilities, which I then attacked to remedy. It was a holistic approach. You can't improve one area while ignoring another. I learned that *everything is everything*. If you want to improve your health, but you think tackling your business is more important, you'll soon discover it doesn't work like that. Everything has to be worked on at once because they all overlap. They are inextricably connected because they are all *you*.

Everything overlaps—and whatever you work on within yourself will translate into how you do everything. It made me a better person. My goals changed, and I could finally hear my higher, authentic, best self.

In 2015, after a few years of deep inner work, I felt more confident in taking the plunge into entrepreneurship to build Rastegar. I vowed to create a better way to do business in real estate, a more human approach mixed with extensive data. We peel the onion every day to improve as an organization. Business is a team sport. Everyone must play their position. Choose your team wisely, because in most instances, you spend more time with them than you do with your own family.

If I hadn't taken the time to work on myself prior to launching Rastegar, I doubt the business would be successful. I live by the Japanese philosophy called *kaizen*, or *continuous improvement*. Tony Robbins calls it CANI—Constant And Never-Ending Improvement. I like to add, "Till the day I die."

YOU ARE AN EXTENSION OF YOUR BUSINESS

There's a common phrase in the business world: "How you do anything is how you do everything." It's a brilliant philosophy to adjust your mindset. How you deal with yourself is a reflection of how you deal with your business. *You* are the core foundation.

The question is, why would anyone want to do business with *you*? It's not because you have the next hottest product or service. It has much less to do with the numbers on a spreadsheet than you may think. At the end of the product or service, there is a human being. As a general rule, customers make buying decisions based on the company's core values. As Simon Sinek says, "People don't buy what you do. They buy why you do it."

It all boils down to *who you are.*

Is there integrity around the product you're creating? Is the product something consumers genuinely need? Are you truly creating value? Are you personally in love with what you're selling?

I often joke with friends that I've never seen a pitch book that says the project is going to lose money—but it certainly happens! The client is betting on the jockey. Better said, they are investing in the person, the team, and the beliefs behind the idea. Projections are rarely reached in real life; projections are another word for assumptions. We know what happens when we *assume* things. The target goal is either surpassed or underachieved. Instead, clients assess you and your ability to make those numbers happen. Do you have the energy, passion, and conviction to do what's necessary? Can they feel deep, undeniable belief in the efficacy of your product? You can't fake authenticity. Consumers are not stupid; they need to believe in you. This means you need to believe in yourself even more.

ACCOUNTABILITY

My advice is to have someone hold you accountable. You can pick a friend, partner, mentor, a personal coach, anyone that you know will hold you to your promises. There are plenty of free services out there to accommodate. A gem of wisdom is to choose someone so annoying that they will happily call you out, lovingly. Don't pick the roll-over friend. I like financial consequences. If you miss the gym, you pay your accountability partner. The consequence is key.

> Life coaches are there to call you out when you're being ridiculous and to help you set up the conditions to reach your goals.

You might balk at hiring a coach, but most (if not all) professionals have one. Every athlete, musician, and successful entrepreneur has someone. Tim Grover couldn't play one-on-one with Michael Jordan, but he was the one to point out his mistakes and guide him along a path of improvement.

If you're early into your career and don't have the means yet, there are several other ways for you to work on yourself. Start with some self-reflection and introspection. And please, read. Then read more. Listen to a podcast. Have insatiable curiosity to grow and learn from those who came before you and model their success.

I learned the hard way. I believe the following five points represent personal characteristics that are vital in running a successful business. These are the *intangibles*.

PERSONAL INTEGRITY

The promises you make to other people are vital, of course. Although, the most important ones are making and keeping the promises to yourself.

It took me a while to understand the difference. I thought personal integrity was upholding your promises to other people. I came to understand the truth: we keep promises to other people because they have inherent consequences. For example, if I make a commitment to someone and don't follow through, they'll think I'm a flake and unreliable. Since I don't want them to think that, I fulfill my obligation.

That's keeping a promise to someone else, not to ourselves.

We don't keep the promises we make to ourselves because there's nobody to hold us accountable. How many times have you told yourself that you're going to go to the gym but then don't? Or that you're going to order a salad next time you go out to eat, but then order junk food instead? I know I have!

We don't think these little moments matter, but they absolutely do. "The little things are the big things," as you have heard ad nauseam. When you don't keep the promises you make to yourself, you personify that inner voice inside your head, and that inner voice starts to judge you. The more you cancel on yourself, the more that inner voice dislikes you. After countless broken promises, it now starts to think you're unreliable, and treats you as such. I believe this is the root cause of the epidemic of a lack of self-love and self-respect we are suffering from as a global society. You have only yourself to blame. You're the one responsible for cultivating that damaging, negative inner dialogue. And that is the good news, because it means *you* are in control.

When I first started working on myself, I realized that I wasn't good at keeping promises I made to myself, much less knowing which promises I should be making in the first place.

I unveiled a profound flaw that gave me something concrete to work on. I chalked up being ultra-hard on myself (to the point of unproductivity) to a lack of focus. Doctors tried to prescribe me ADHD medication to help control my hyperactivity, and antianxiety pharmaceuticals from what they diagnosed as a symptom of "my intense workload." Instead of addressing the root cause, they wanted to medicate me. "You don't need any of that," Lauren said. "It all has to do with the inner dialogue you have with yourself." She was right.

This was a shocking revelation. I never liked the idea of taking pharmaceuticals. I always thought them to be mere bandages, and now I was ready to address the root cause and cure it. This was a personal revolution that when conquered would lead to the greatest breakthrough of my life, thus far. I was all in.

Instead of medicine, I tracked and documented my inner dialogue to see how I spoke to myself—what words I used, what tone I used, what thoughts ran through my head, and focused on the fundamentals. As Don Meyer says, "To win it all, winners have to be obsessive about the fundamentals and doing the little things right."

Focusing on the fundamentals was something I'd never done

before, and it ended up being a phenomenal exercise—one that I highly recommend you explore. I'll give you the disclaimer now: It can get quite boring. Embrace it. Study the greats in any arena. They are all experts in the fundamentals. All of them. No exceptions. Trust the process.

AUTHENTICITY

"Authenticity requires a certain measure of vulnerability, transparency, and integrity."

—JANET LOUISE STEPHENSON

When I was growing up, I always wanted to blend in. I wanted to root for the same sports teams as my friends, or to wear the same fashionable clothes. During my deep dive of introspection, I started to really listen to my *authentic* voice. I quickly understood that I viewed the world through a different lens. I think that's true of everyone. Once you do the introspection and start to hear your own voice, you'll find the truth, the value, and the beauty in what *you* think, not what the world is telling you to think. By doing so, you will find your authentic voice. It might be a whisper, but trust me, it is there. The more you give it attention, the more it will grow. As you begin to give attention or energy to anything, focus will amplify—as will the results.

I encourage you to listen to yourself. We often value other people's opinions more than we value our own, which is preposterous if you really think about it. No one knows you like you. You need to look at yourself, listen, honor your thoughts, and you will find your truth. Trust that what is in you is holy, valuable, and a true expression of your calling in life.

It's in you. Have you ever read a quote for the first time and found yourself acknowledging the truth in it? It's as if you already knew the truth of those words, even though you've never thought about them before. You think to yourself, *I already knew that.* That goes back to this place of your authentic self. Deep down inside, you already knew that truth. When you give advice to your friends or family, you're sharing insight based on your experience, your knowledge, and your authentic self. We need to do the same for ourselves. Practice giving yourself advice, and practice taking it. It's hard at first, but you get better at it, just like you would when learning any other skill. Keep on keeping on.

For that to happen, however, you'll need to allow yourself an excruciating amount of vulnerability. It's tough.

VULNERABILITY

"To share your weakness is to make yourself vulnerable; to make yourself vulnerable is to show strength."

—CRISS JAMI

You'll have to be vulnerable to look at yourself with the level of introspection needed to examine your flaws and mistakes. You *must* be vulnerable. It's a monster pill that will make you choke. You *almost* can't swallow it. But almost doesn't count. Be like Yoda: "Do or do not. There is no try." It took an incredible level of vulnerability to stand in front of myself, both literally and figuratively, where I saw my cracks, my flaws, and all my shortcomings. It was a genuine step towards letting go of my ego. I experienced the definition of the word *bittersweet.* I learned in law school that a good attorney should be able to fight for both sides, take an objective look at all arguments, and leave out emotion. So that's what I did. I took a bird's eye view of myself, depersonalized the equation, and found the truth. Vulnerability is human, it's powerful, and it translates into confidence. But it hurts, at first.

Personally, it was excruciatingly painful.

I recommend watching Brené Brown's TED Talk: "The Power of Vulnerability." Watch it intently, twice, and back-to-back. It's mind-blowing, beautiful, and powerful. I watch it often still—it's one of the ways I engrain the fundamentals deep into my psyche.

I'm gradually learning to be uncomfortable—because I know that's where the most growth happens. It's like pushing through your last rep at the gym. When your muscles are burning and want to give out by the eighth rep, you need to push through the discomfort and finish the set because those last reps are where the most results happen. This is the natural law of physics and psychology, and we need to push through to get a breakthrough.

That moment is miserable. It's full of pain, fear, and discomfort. But when you come out on the other side, not only are you relieved, but you'll feel elated that you did it. You tackled it. You conquered it. Perhaps, you even look back and think it wasn't that bad in the first place. Oh wait, it *was* that bad. But I can breathe.

I started to learn to accept discomfort around 2010, when I was reintroduced to the ancient practice of yoga. I was blessed that the universe guided me to Nevine Michaan, the creator of Katonah Yoga, a marriage of Taoism principles, yoga, and sacred geometry. Nevine is one of the most incredible human beings I've ever met, and she told me something that still resonates. During one of our practices, I struggled to move gracefully from pose to pose, sweating, shaking, and gritting my teeth. When we finished, I sat a little longer to compose myself, breathe, and just be. She came over to sit with me and said, "It takes a whole lot of effort to become effortless." When you watch a professional golfer's swing, it looks effortless and beautiful; that's because they spent hours upon hours putting in the effort to become effortless.

She might have been talking about yoga, but just like all truth, it applies to everything in life, so that's what I did. I applied it.

THE BIRTH OF RASTEGAR

In 2015, while Kellie gave birth to our second child, Kingston (or as his older sister says, "Mr. King-King"), I gave birth to what evolved into Rastegar.

At first, as with most entrepreneurial starts, it was just me. I did *everything*. For eighteen hours a day (I'm being painfully conservative), I was responsible for finding the clients, assessing the opportunities, working on the legal, and even doing the janitorial work. It was not out of the ordinary to sleep in the office—not on purpose but out of necessity! It was like trying to push a battleship while swimming. I was all alone in the office, putting in an extraordinary amount of work and persisting to get the firm off the ground.

Before my introspection, my inner dialogue was magnificently damaging. If I had an idea, my inner voice would quickly shoot it down. *That's stupid. You're not Bill Gates, so any idea coming from you won't be that good*—so on and so on, getting progressively worse and worse. Practice and repetition helped me tame that negative inner voice, enabling me to believe in myself in a new way and to learn the true meaning of personal integrity. I created my own constitution—or simply a set of rules and consequences to live by (thank you, Lauren). This change along with my newfound confidence gave me the tools I needed to tackle the next stage of my life.

Capital A was a great idea, but it was someone else's idea. Working in the entertainment industry in that capacity didn't reflect a deep, authentic inner desire of mine; it didn't reflect my lifelong purpose or speak to my authentic self. That said, in hindsight, while the experience was a "failure," learning about the entertainment business—and namely how to serve clients with supreme customer service—gave me an edge to better serve my future clients with a higher standard of care.

As I started to listen to myself, I asked different questions, better questions. A respected acquaintance of mine, Jay Abraham, said something profound: "Questions are the answer. So ask the right question if you want the right answer."

By now, I had worked in real estate private equity for several years, but I wanted to do things differently. Was there a better way to do this? Was there a better way to design and build? To operate? To treat clients, vendors, and staff?

In other words, how can *I* be better?

With those questions in mind, I recalled the business motto of my dear family friend, Randal LeBlanc: "Ari, don't reinvent the wheel, but just keep it balanced and aligned." That meant to do ordinary tasks in an extraordinary manner.

Rastegar was mission-driven from inception. Our mission was to focus on holistic real estate projects that cater to and serve the lifestyle of the modern world and the people that inhabit it.

There are several ways to value a business, most of which are tangible and have to do with financials, like tallying up the value of the business's assets, and subtracting liabilities. What most people fail to consider are the intangibles, like culture and the humanity of the company. To me, once you start your business, *you* are your most important asset. Remember, as you build yourself, you'll also build your business.

CHAPTER 3

YOU ARE YOUR MOST IMPORTANT ASSET

"You cannot dream yourself into a character; you must hammer and forge yourself one."

—HENRY DAVID THOREAU

Launching a business is like riding a bike—the only way to learn is to ride.

While I worked in getting Rastegar off the ground, I had to be the entrepreneur and the dealmaker—two different responsibilities that require very separate skill sets. I was learning while I was working.

Meanwhile at home, my role as both a husband and a parent required me to be available. From watching over our firstborn to going out on grocery runs or fixing a bottle, there was always a new demand for my time. It was a crazy amount of responsibility for one person to bear, but I did the best that I could, and I was willing to do whatever it took to be there for my growing family. After all, servitude was my focus, and this gave me a silent energy reserve to keep going.

I knew my *why* would pull me to the goal and that my *what* would push me—that all this wasn't about just building a business; it was about building a life.

Ralph Waldo Emerson said, "There is a time in every man's education when he arrives at the conviction that envy is ignorance; that imitation is suicide; that he must take himself for better, for worse, as his portion." This applies to all people. I needed to be *better*—a better entrepreneur, a better family member, a better friend. In short, a better human being. I wasn't out to just make money. It wasn't just about me. I wanted to make my ancestors and future bloodline proud. I wanted to save future generations of my family from the struggle I endured and provide an opportunity for them to follow their dreams.

Soon the hours and manic hard work started to add up, and I became perpetually—excessively—exhausted. My body struggled to keep up. I was only in my early thirties, but my body didn't perform as well as it once did. When I met with potential clients and venture partners for Rastegar, I wasn't showing up in my usual electric and passionate Ari way. My body and mind started to feel dull and tired. It was subtle, but I noticed. It drove me crazy!

I didn't stop, but everything became harder and harder. I was struggling to retain focus, and instead I caught myself distracted compared to years before. I frequently had to think harder, and double-check my math, which was not normal for me. I was yawning a lot, too. I'd wake up and instead of feeling refreshed from a good night's sleep, I still felt drained. Dark circles started to appear under my eyes. Fatigue affected my appetite, too, and I started to lose weight. I didn't have much weight to lose in the first place, so I started to look feeble.

My abusive inner dialogue said, *Damn, I'm getting old.* My higher self disagreed!

It wasn't like I disregarded taking care of myself, either, despite enjoying the occasional French fries (one my favorites, extra crispy). I have always been conscious of my health, thanks in part to my parents who instilled in me knowledge about health and fitness. In fact, my mother was a homeopath, and before my father became an attorney, he was a massage therapist. They were both vegetarians for fifteen years before it was fashionable. Our house didn't contain many processed foods, and they always emphasized the importance of hydration. Water was our drink of choice instead of soda, juice, or alcohol. Healthy eating was (and continues to be) part of my DNA. This includes taking vitamins, which was always standard practice in our home—then and now.

Despite knowing better, I chose to ignore what my body was telling me. I worked harder and harder, slept less and less, and continued to feel worse inside. *Failure.*

After several weeks of what seemed like nonstop yawning and sluggishness, I decided to see a doctor. Maybe they could shed some light on why I felt so tired all the time. Was I not sleeping as well? Was I under too much pressure? Was I too stressed? I already knew the answer to those questions (probably—yes), but I wanted to see if there were any underlying conditions. When I saw a doctor, his solution was to prescribe me a sleeping pill for my fatigue and Xanax for my stress.

Um...no thanks. Again!

I wasn't looking for pills to fix me. Instead, I turned to self-help books, breathing techniques, and a lot of prayer. I wanted to address the root problem of why I was expending so much energy to keep up with the growing demands of creating and launching my new life. My intuition told me I was missing something.

And I was. I was desperate, which is still hard for me to admit. I wanted to change. I needed to change.

And then I found meditation. I can't thank the universe enough for this gift that keeps on giving.

I didn't just find your standard, run-of-the-mill meditation (although almost all types of meditation are beneficial). I discovered Transcendental Meditation, or TM, a specific form of mantra-based meditation. It was reintroduced by Maharishi Mahesh Yogi. He was educated in physics and quantum mechanics and a Vedic teacher whose practice of meditation illuminated and simplified an ancient Vedic technology. Maharishi explained TM as a technology, which drew me in. I especially loved the sheer quantity of scholarly research and science proving the validity and benefits of the practice.

TM wasn't new to me. In fact, my stepfather, who married my mother when I was three, was an avid meditator. I just didn't realize what it was at the time.

As an adult, TM seemed to appear often in my life, waving its hands so I would take notice. My longtime friend Mitch Lewis recommended it, and I'd heard many celebrities and influencers—like Jerry Seinfeld, Ellen DeGeneres, Howard Stern, the Beatles, and a slew of other ultra-high performers in all industries—tout the success Transcendental Meditation had on them. They said it reduced their stress, decreased their blood pressure, and improved their sleeping, brain function, and memory. Some people even claimed that it helped them conquer their addiction to cigarettes and alcohol. Bold. I liked it.

Despite my exposure to it, I never thought to pursue it.

It wasn't until I watched an interview with the larger-than-life Raymond "Ray" Dalio, an American billionaire who founded Bridgewater Associates, the largest hedge fund company in the world. To say I admired him would be an understatement. From all my studies of Dalio, it appeared he did life right. His 2017 philosophy book, *Principles: Life & Work,* had a huge influence on me. It was originally released for free on his website years before being formally published, which a friend printed and gave to me. I downloaded and read it in full in a single night—years before he published the book itself. Do yourself a favor and read it, study it. Then do it again. I wouldn't be offended if you put this book down to read that one. It is special.

As I watched the interview, I fixated on his answers, hanging on his every word. At one point, the reporter asked him, "If you could narrow down all the things that you did to reach your success, what would you pinpoint as the *most* important thing?"

Ray Dalio's answer: "Transcendental Meditation."

Huh? That was the last thing I expected to come out of his mouth. This individual is extraordinary—we're talking about one of the most successful and most ethical investors in the world. In my eyes, he is the sage of all stock market sages, and instead of listing a life-changing book, or an influential mentor, he openly proclaimed that TM was *the* X factor.

I needed to give it a try.

"Let's do this together," I said to Kellie. I found a school in Dallas that offered a three-day TM course for beginners and signed us up. The point of the course was to teach students so that they could implement and practice at home. Our teacher, Ron, was instrumental in turning our lives around, and he's still a dear friend to this day.

Mantra-based meditation is effectively a mind technique, and truly a technology. People see meditation through various preconceived notions such as spirituality, maybe religion, or a variety of other perceptions. TM is a technique to achieve physiological benefits using your own mind. The technique upgrades you, in myriad ways, and I can vouch for this first-hand. It's between you and you. It doesn't require any special equipment or gear. It's about focusing your most subtle attention on a sound. The instructor gives you a mantra (the sound), and you repeat it for twenty minutes twice a day through a process that is natural and simple. There's no set order or number of repetitions. Without hyperbole, after that first night, I felt like I took a breath of fresh air for the first time in decades.

The process was effortless, which is what I loved about it most. In the real world, I'm always *doing* something. Meditation offers a release. It gives me the opportunity to slow down. During TM, I am simply being. As I sit fully aware of my alert, yet quiet, stillness, repeating my mantra, it's as if time stops. I come out of it feeling refreshed, invigorated, and ready. After all, meditation is used to prepare for action, not to "relax"—a common misconception.

TM is personal and intimate in nature. I won't share the mantras the course taught us (because they're confidential), but the fact is it works. And to my pleasant surprise, it keeps getting better and better.

After the three-day course, Kellie and I applied what we learned and started practicing at home. As instructed, I did it twice daily for twenty minutes, and within days I saw a stark improvement in my fatigue. I slept better and felt more refreshed in the mornings. The bags under my eyes disappeared. My appetite returned, and I started eating consistently again, gaining healthy weight back. I even stopped yawning as much. I felt invigorated, and it started to show in my work. I had more energy and deeper focus. Mentally speaking, I felt more grounded. I even cracked a smile here and there, which was rare in those days, embarrassingly enough. Following your dreams is not all candy canes and lollipops.

I now understand why Ray Dalio called TM the key to his accomplishments. When I met him for the first time, I told him about my experience, and his eyes lit up. "It only gets better," he said. His eyes told the whole story and validated everything as fact, not placebo. I was on cloud nine! I will never forget that moment for the rest of my life.

I highly recommend you find a local TM Center and take the three-day course (which is only one hour per day for three days). I would venture to say it will be one of the greatest gifts you will ever give to yourself. My gratitude for this technology is boundless.

Now don't get me wrong, this wasn't a magic pill. I still had other health issues to resolve (which we'll get to in Chapter 5).

INVEST IN YOURSELF

"Personal development: the never-ending chance to improve not only yourself, but also to attract opportunities and affect others."

—JIM ROHN

Starting any business is a risk financially, but more so personally. While it's imperative to build and take care of your business assets, entrepreneurs often forget about their most important one: themselves. You are your business's biggest asset, so treat yourself as such. Your business will not grow without you, so while investing in your company is important, you simply cannot neglect investing in yourself. You must take care of all facets of yourself before you are ready to pour the foundation. Like I said, you are the foundation. As Maharishi Mahesh Yogi once said: "You have to water the root to enjoy the fruit."

Personal development is the way. It includes anything that you do to improve. This can mean many things, from reading books, prayer, attending seminars, exercising, to learning new skills. Anything that continuously allows you to learn, evolve, adapt, and to constructively feel alive falls under this broad umbrella. The essence is growth and contribution.

Everyone will have a different definition of what this means. Personally, it comes down to one thing: expansion. Are you consciously expanding your mind? Your limits? Your body? Whether you're learning proper exercise techniques, financial tools to better save for the future, or new vocabulary words from all the reading you're doing, you are expanding. You are growing. Mix that with contribution beyond yourself, and therein lies the proverbial "secret sauce" to wild outlandish success and fulfillment.

> Instead of mercilessly pushing myself to the brink of exhaustion. I learned to seek new ways to expand myself to be more self-aware. And when my tactics don't work, I fail quickly, readjust, analyze, and hit it again with improvements.

The more you take care of yourself, the more energy you'll have to serve others. Many people depend on me, and they depend on me to be my best self. This is my honor and privilege. My work is my worship. It is who I am, not what I do.

When you fly on an airplane, the flight attendants remind passengers that in the event the cabin pressure drops, you should put the mask on yourself first before helping others.[1] That analogy can be applied to our lives. Take care of yourself first so you can effectively take care of others. If you don't put yourself first, you won't have the energy to help those who need you. Do this humbly, not selfishly.

Meditation is just one beneficial avenue in self-improvement. A quick Google search will explain why it is good for you. Most are backed by scientific studies, but in general, meditation enhances empathy, improves cognition, is a stress stabilizer, promotes emotional health, enhances self-awareness, and can even reduce age-related memory loss.

There are a ton of ways to meditate; it really boils down to personal preference. I will say this: you don't have to jump into twenty-minute sessions right away. If you're new to meditation, take it slow. Start by meditating for two minutes. I don't care how busy you are, anyone can spare two minutes. If you don't have two minutes to yourself, you don't have control over your life. Once you've established a routine to meditate for two minutes, increase it to three minutes. Build upon your meditation practice just like you would build your business: one step at a time. Before you know it, you'll be increasing the length of your sessions and reaping all the benefits—and so will your business.

PERSONAL DEVELOPMENT FOR A BETTER YOU

"To understand the universe, think in terms of energy, wavelengths, and frequency."

—NIKOLA TESLA

MENTORSHIP IN PEOPLE *AND* IN BOOKS

When most people think of mentorship, they think of a Mr. Miyagi-type character passing on knowledge and expertise to someone usually younger or less experienced.

Although this is accurate—and beneficial—I look at mentorship through a different lens. Mentorship, in essence, is modeling or mimicking the behavior of those you respect, heeding the advice that serves your mission, and ignoring the rest. I've had a plethora of face-to-face mentors throughout my life. I've also found mentorship through people I've never met or spoken to. Many of my favorites are characters in books—or the authors themselves.

Anyone who I greatly admired and was dedicated to greatness became a mentor. Whether I admired them due to their business acumen, their creativity, or their athletic aptitude, I studied them, particularly athletes, because their abilities are on full display in real time. I especially enjoy studying Serena Williams, Tom Brady, Muhammad Ali, Lionel Messi, Michael Phelps, Roger Federer, Kobe Bryant, and Simone Biles, because the fundamentals of discipline are the same in athletics as in business. I read about them and learned what they did every day that led them to their success. If applicable, I'd adopt their habits to see if they would help me. At the very least, they became sources of motivation and inspiration to continue my journey of training for life and working to be fit for business.

Find people who are doing what you want to be doing and study them. What do they do daily? What are the habits and behaviors that they implemented? Model their success and dissect their failures. If you admire a businesswoman who's made millions, what habits and behaviors contributed to her success? By finding people who are experiencing the things that you want to experience, you can learn from them and begin to adopt and implement the same habits and actions. You might even learn new skills to help expand your own awareness. Don't fear rejection; embrace it. Reach out. It is now easier than ever through social media and email to get to those people directly. It just takes some courage and a burning desire to achieve your wildest dreams—which you will. Just follow the rules and don't skip steps. Elon Musk started his own business after he was rejected to work at Netscape.

Reading autobiographies has been an incredible source of mentorship. Learning about the lives of those who came before us offer a multitude of lessons and wisdom. Reading about their struggles, their successes, and even the little serendipitous things that happened to them have been guiding lights. The human condition endures, and you will be pleasantly surprised to see your fears are not unique to you. This offers an awkward element of comfort on the lonely journey to the top.

One of my favorites to examine and reexamine is Benjamin Franklin. The breadth of what he accomplished is simply astounding—from inventing bifocal eyeglasses to making several discoveries involving electricity to cofounding the United States of America. The man is an inspiration. He's like America's Leonardo da Vinci (I don't make that comparison lightly). His life further amazes me, considering he lived in a time when life expectancy was half of what it is now (even though he did live a fairly long life). As a polymath, he also documented his life meticulously, leaving us with a better understanding of what it was like during his time.

I garnered several lessons from Franklin (some to do and others not to do), like taking audacious goals and breaking them down into smaller, more digestible goals; some call it "chunking." With all that he accomplished, it appears that Franklin didn't succumb to procrastination, which is something I aspire to. When approaching new ideas, he'd create a list with its pros and cons, weighing each side to see if it was worthy of pursuit. These are all things I've adopted.

Books are my fundamental and preferred resource for learning. I urge you to discover how you learn best. Nothing is more powerful than the treasure of knowledge, and the way to acquire this is to learn as you can. If you choose to read like I do, which I highly recommend, be sure to read with a pen and take note of the important passages. Science has established that the more senses you employ during learning, the easier it is to lock the knowledge into your long-term memory. Reading books is an easy and affordable way to invest in yourself. I love to buy and read used books; sometimes there's even knowledge in the notes from the previous owner! Don't forget the many resources available for free in your public library. Check out the list of recommended reading in the appendix if you're looking for more insight.

FINDING THE RIGHT SENSORY INPUT

Utilizing a variety of different sensory inputs improves learning efficiency. Reading is one way to digest information, but there are several other ways depending on personal preference—such as listening to audiobooks and podcasts or watching videos and documentaries. Cultivate self-awareness and take the time to discover how *you* learn best. It is not the same for everyone.

If you don't enjoy reading, try audiobooks which are easily accessible online. A significant benefit of listening to audiobooks (and podcasts, for that matter) is that this format allows you to learn while doing something else. I'm not a fan of what is traditionally called "multitasking"; I think it hinders deep learning. However, anytime you are exposed to great minds and new ideas, there is a tremendous benefit. When it comes to multimedia, we have access to a staggering amount of free information. Some of it can be total garbage, so spend time to find quality content. It is there!

Learning is inspiring and motivating. Lean in, enjoy the process! As an example, TED Talks has expanded and is always releasing new content. I have an ever-growing list of favorites that I revisit and learn something new each time. You can learn just about anything, from quantum physics to Mozart to crypto trading. Learn, learn, and learn more. Never stop learning! The process of learning is an opportunity to change behaviors and upgrade habits. *Unlearning*, or letting go of inaccurate information or unhelpful habits, is arguably more important than learning. Erase the old software and install the new. Just like your cell phone, make sure to get the updates! True learning requires un-learning. To do otherwise is shortsighted, or at least counterproductive.

Personally, I'm a reader. I watch videos and listen to podcasts too, but I prefer to read. I like it because it taps into more of my senses. Maybe it's the English major in me; maybe it's because both my parents were always reading. I like feeling the weight of the book in my hand and flipping through the pages. I like seeing the ink of the sans serif font and the color choices of the front cover. I like the smell of the pages. I'm also an active reader, meaning I highlight, underline, and write in my books. I'm actively engaging with the words and the physical form of the book. These multiple active touchpoints help digest the information into my long-term memory. Public libraries used to frown upon my notes in the margins. They called it "defacing materials," and I had to buy a lot of those books back.

I read constantly. Any spare moment in my day, I try to fill it with reading. I read in micro chunks, even if it's just a page or a sentence. I don't always read them sequentially. I'll flip to a random section and read it. I'll read a few pages when I wake up, before bed, while riding in a car, or while waiting for a flight. When traveling, I pack books before clothes.

People complain they don't have time to read. C'mon. We all have the same twenty-four hours in a day. If that's your excuse, a free course on time management will serve you well. I'm busy too. I get it. You don't have to dedicate hours upon hours of uninterrupted reading. Do what I do and read in chunks. Read one page a day. Hell, one paragraph a day. As the saying goes, "Small hinges swing big doors." However you do it, just do it. Be consistent and unwavering. Your dedication will compound, and results will follow.

Take that approach with everything. Don't overextend with

unrealistic expectations. Wishful thinking and goals are not the same. Tiny goals are great goals. Go small, go slow, and build momentum. Momentum is a force that rivals gravity. Focus on making minor, manageable micro changes. Make your goal so easy that any excuse not to do it would be embarrassing. I'm not asking you to run a marathon tomorrow. I'm not asking you to read a book in three days. Make small changes that easily incorporate into your routine—micro changes that compound in the long run. Meditate for one minute a day for a week. Increase it to two minutes the next week. Breathe deeply for ten seconds, and then increase that to twenty seconds. Read a paragraph out of a book while you're waiting for your coffee to heat up. Set yourself up for success. All wins build momentum and will take you further than you can imagine.

> Don't tell me you're busy. We are all busy. You can spare two minutes out of your day to meditate or read a page out of a book.

We make time for what we value. If you don't have two minutes, then you need to reevaluate your entire existence on this planet. I have a sneaky suspicion you *do* have time; you just have to prioritize yourself.

NEVER-ENDING PURSUIT

"Become addicted to constant and never-ending self-improvement."
—ANTHONY J. D'ANGELO

You are your most important asset. Improvement is a life-long practice. You are all you have. New habits don't come easy but can be developed, cultivated, and grown. I'm constantly evolving, fine-tuning, and making mistakes (more than I care to admit).

Cornerstone habits should come first. These, like exercise and proper nutrition, improve more than just one facet of life. They have resounding holistic benefits. When you take good care of yourself, you'll see improvements in nearly all aspects of life.

Reading and absorbing information is great. But it won't stick permanently unless you put your body into it. What I mean by that is putting your heart, soul, and mind into integrating these practices into your daily life. You must become the practice.

At first, I did not understand this. That was my failure. The reasons don't matter. What matters is that now I know—and so will you.

CHAPTER 4

PUT YOUR BODY
INTO IT

"Success is the product of the severest kind of mental and physical application."

—THOMAS A. EDISON

If you don't put what you learn into use, then the idea is just a thought and not actionable. To transmute your goal into reality, you must *put your body into it.* When I say put your body into it, I mean take your thoughts, ideas, dreams and literally use your body to project them out into the universe. Write it, yell it, and demand it!

My journey of putting my body into it started with a book. My *baba* (dad) gave me *Think and Grow Rich* by Napoleon Hill when I was thirteen years old.

"Here," he said, handing me the book in the kitchen of our duplex in University Park, Texas. Baba was a few inches taller than me, fifty pounds heavier, a fifth-degree black belt, and an all-around tough guy. A very loving man, but stringent with core values. As a father myself, I'm still in awe of how much he effortlessly taught me.

His philosophy embodied the Mark Twain quote, "I never let schooling interfere with my education." He was unwavering in providing a world-class education, ensuring that I learned in and out of the public school system. I was used to him constantly handing me books to read. This time was different.

"What's this?" I asked.

"This is one of the most important books you'll ever read," he said with a smile. He was so adamant about me reading this particular book, at this particular time. Based on his tone, I had no choice but to read it. There was an unusual sparkle in his eye. I was intrigued, and immediately went to my room.

The opening sentence blew me away: "Truly, 'thoughts are things,' and powerful things at that, when they are mixed with definiteness of purpose, persistence, and a burning desire for their translation into riches, or other material objects."

Whoa. I was hooked.

The first chapters were a visceral experience. I was both elated and scared. Overflowing with questions, I rushed downstairs to discuss them with Baba. "Is this guy for real?" I asked. His response triggered one of the most memorable conversations we ever had.

"Napoleon Hill spent over twenty years interviewing the

richest men in America and distilled their universal wisdom into one book," my dad told me. Mr. Hill interviewed J.P. Morgan, Andrew Carnegie, Thomas Edison, and John D. Rockefeller, just to name a few notables. His remarkable discovery was the similarities between all their habits, thoughts, and routines.

"The introduction opens with the phrase, 'Thoughts are things.' What does that even mean, Baba?"

"It means that what you *think*, you are. Period. The key to success is first understanding that we have the power to control our thoughts—then taking responsibility for doing so. If we choose not to control our thoughts, they end up controlling us."

Baba furthered explained that thoughts determine whether we succeed or fail. If we choose to fill our minds with thoughts of success, we can achieve riches. It was a formula more than a philosophy. It was practical, repeatable, and clearly effective.

I certainly did not comprehend the implications of the book, but the words resonated with me, and a seed was planted. Obviously, as a thirteen-year-old boy, I didn't apply everything I learned. Hell, I'm still not applying everything today! But on that day, my world expanded.

I reread the book a few years later at the age of sixteen. (I've since read it at least a hundred times, and it's usually sitting on my desk or somewhere close by.) Mr. Hill presents a formula in how to set and achieve goals. In his own words, "Your only limitation is the one you set up in your own mind."

With this newfound inspiration, I wrote down a goal: I am a billionaire. (Yes, great goals are written in the present tense.)

I wanted to be a billionaire to have a voice and a platform. Maybe then I could help bring positive change to the world. But first, I had to change myself. Simon Sinek stated, "People don't buy what you do. They buy why you do it." The *why* behind my goal was greatly rooted in my upbringing. Not only were there times of financial struggle, especially as a kid, but I wanted to honor my family. I wanted to build a legacy, and through it help others. That is all I knew.

I certainly didn't have a plan on how I was going to reach that goal. Taking Mr. Hill's words to heart, I had faith and wrote it down anyway. In fact, I wrote myself a check for a billion dollars, dated it ten years into the future, and carried it around with me as a constant reminder.

As college approached, Baba laid out clear expectations: "You're going to be an attorney. Playtime is over. From here on, it all counts."

At first, I chuckled. "I don't want to be an attorney." I wasn't the best student in high school, so what made him think I could be an attorney?

"Ariah," he said sternly. "After becoming an attorney, you can be an exotic dancer for all I care!"

Baba didn't care if I wanted to practice law; he just wanted me to have something to work toward. As an attorney, he knew becoming one would offer a concrete path, which was more important than *not* having one.

It was decided—and thank goodness it was because I didn't know any better. It reminded me of a quote from Mark Twain: "When I was fourteen, I didn't realize how little my father knew about the world. When I turned twenty-one, I couldn't believe how much he learned in seven years"—except for me, the timeframe occurred between ages eighteen and twenty-six.

Even though I had no desire to work in law, I loved my father dearly, and trusted him (and was moderately scared of him). I did as instructed. In retrospect, it was a gift. My other option was to join the Army, but that is a story for another time. He was guiding me before I knew how to guide myself. I didn't have clear direction, and he knew I wouldn't have acted if he didn't lay down the law, so to speak.

> Either you set your goals or the world will set them for you. Thanks to Baba, this was failure averted.

Before law school, I had to get my undergrad. I screwed up the SATs, because I walked out in the middle. Baba was not pleased. So, I attended two community colleges (Richland Community College in Dallas, and Blinn Community College in Bryan, Texas) before being accepted to Texas A&M University. Thank goodness for Richland and Blinn because they prepared me for what came next.

Baba expected me to major in finance or business. His preference was accounting, the "language of business." But as I scrolled through the list of majors, English caught my eye.

English? As a major? What does that even entail? I looked over the list of classes required to earn the degree, and even glanced over a few sample syllabi. It was basically a long list of books and essay assignments.

I just have to read all these books? I was stoked. I had already read many of them. Thinking it would be easy, I chose to major in English.

I took the path of least resistance, so I thought. Majoring in English was much harder than I anticipated. In fact, it was far more challenging than law school for me—especially since studying was a skill that I had yet to learn.

English ended up being a strong choice. It helped me become a better thinker and taught me patience. Patience was a virtue I lacked. Reading and analyzing books during my undergrad years made me more creative and imaginative. It also elevated my critical thinking skills, which were extremely useful during law school. For example, when a law assignment required us to read a case and summarize, I looked at it as if I was reading a story and then summarized the themes, conflict, and characters.

During law school, I thought about what I wanted for myself. I loved reading and writing, *and* I had a passion for art. I thought about pursuing a career in the movie business. I set my eyes on Hollywood, never forgetting the dream to own all the tall buildings.

USING YOUR BODY

There are many ways to use your body when it comes to realizing your goals. Here are a few that have worked for me:

WRITE YOUR GOALS DOWN ON PAPER

Goal setting isn't simply imagining what you want. It is a technique that converts dreams into reality. *Write them down.* That's the secret. It takes a thought and literally makes it concrete. Now that it is on paper, it is not just a thought; it is tangible.

When building a skyscraper, you must take a thought and create a *blueprint.* Hence, putting your idea to paper. School is no different. You get a syllabus—effectively a blueprint—a goal in chunks, with a clear result: a degree. This law is universal. The formula is the same for achieving any goal.

Until it's written down on paper, it's simply wishful thinking.

AFFIRMATIONS

"I am the greatest. I said that even before I knew I was."

—MUHAMMAD ALI

Think you're destined to fail, and you will. But believe you're in charge of your own success and you'll achieve your dreams. The way we speak to ourselves conditions our belief systems—which affect how we see the world. An affirmation is a way to alter your mindset to prime it for success.

Affirmations are short statements of something you aim to

possess or embody. They are declarations of what you *want* to be true about yourself. You write them in the present tense, as if they were already true. Some examples include:

- I am creative. I am compassionate. I am loving.
- I am happy. I am healthy. I am full of energy.
- I feed my spirit. I train my body. It's my time to give.

Using affirmations is a proven way to reprogram your thought process and shift your paradigm into that of the person you *want to be*. To use affirmations effectively, you've got to repeat them *a lot*. I recommend repeating the affirmations out loud in the morning and before bed. To make your affirmations exceptionally powerful, perform them *actively* by using your body. *Active* affirmations reverberate throughout the body and mind. It works. Try it.

I don't know Floyd Mayweather personally, but he is one of the greatest boxers in history. He intensely proclaimed affirmations while he trained—adding another tool to his already formidable tool belt. *You can't touch me. I'm too quick. I'm too strong.* I believe he elevated his performance dramatically by putting his body into those affirmations and repeating the phrases countless times. As the saying goes, "Repetition is the mother of success." This technique was crucial to the longevity of his undefeated career. As the person who landed number one on Forbes' list of "Highest-Paid Athletes of the Decade" at $915 million in December 2019, I'd say he's done quite well for himself.[2]

Like Floyd, repeat your affirmations during exercise. For example, if you're on a run, passionately exclaim your affirmations with each step. You will *feel* the enhancement. It also helps discipline your mind from wanting to quit. Our minds usually try to stop way before our bodies need to. Regardless of your preferred exercise, use your body to express and reinforce your active affirmations.

If you're new to this idea, come up with your own affirmations, or find inspiration online. It's ok to borrow them from others; I certainly have. Eventually you will hear your inner voice. Listen to that whisper as it becomes a scream; it's who you are meant to become. Your affirmation can be whatever you want it to be, whatever resonates with you. Once you have found one that speaks to your heart and soul, scream it at the top of your lungs for all to hear.

Countless experts recommend exclaiming your goals out loud twice a day with passion, faith, and conviction. Do the same with your affirmations. This is not just speaking like you normally do. You need to ROAR! Repeat this two more times throughout the day. Before bed, take time to reflect on how you felt that day. Science shows the time before bed is the most critical time to program your mind with the right data and inputs of your choice. Over time, your desired actions ultimately become habits and deeply ingrained beliefs. After several days, take an inventory of your feelings and notice the improvement. You now are starting to build a priceless blessing: momentum.

I practice affirmations all the time. With my busy schedule, I squeeze them in wherever I can. I'll even do them in the car. I've certainly received some strange looks from other drivers.

I also practice them with my kids sometimes on the way

to school to make sure they are in a confident, intentional mindset. They love doing them and have even come up with their own. *I am kind! I am helpful! I am respectful!* You'd be amazed at how positively it affects them. It's also a fun thing for them to do because, let's be honest, most kids love to yell. I instantly see their self-confidence boost; it brings tears to my eyes just thinking about it.

MANAGE YOUR EMOTIONAL STATE

Our physical attributes dictate our emotional state. If I told you that there was a depressed person in the other room, would you guess they are moving around a lot or not so much? Would they have good posture, or would they be slouched over? Would their speech be upbeat and loud or soft and slow? You'd likely answer that they're not moving much, have hunched shoulders, and are speaking softly and slowly.

The body and the mind are parts of the same continuum. I believe the reason that they're depressed is *because* they're slouched over, not moving around, and speaking slowly. This hypothesis is physiology dictates your mental state, not the other way around. If you want to be happy, you need to move your body, jump up and down, and speak loudly. My yoga teacher, Nevine Michaan, repeatedly said, "You can use your mind to change your body. It is just easier to change your body to change your mind." Powerful.

The first time I did this was at a Tony Robbins conference called Unleash the Power Within. It was an introductory course that he hosted over three days. During one of the sessions, Tony taught his attendees an active affirmation to repeat together:

"Now I am the voice. I will lead, not follow. I will create, not destroy. I'm a source for good. I'm a leader. Defy the odds. Set a new standard. Step up!"

During the conference, he had us scream those phrases at the top of our lungs. Imagine ten thousand people in the Los Angeles Convention Center, yelling that affirmation with the utmost passion. It was electrifying. Not only did I get goosebumps, but I was in tears by the end of it. I was so charged up emotionally that I took it a step further and booked a studio session with a famous music producer in LA. I recorded my goals and several affirmations, and then had them mixed with some music that put me in a good mood. I've listened to it so many times, I've lost count. On the days that I don't do it, I feel the difference—not in a good way!

You don't have to go to a recording studio; you can use your phone to record yourself. Scream your goals and affirmations passionately in the present tense and visualize it all as if it already happened. Feel the gratitude of achieving your dreams, knowing with certainty that they will be your reality.

To further enhance the practice, use *power posing*. What is a power pose? Put your arms up in the air like you just won a race and hold them there! American social psychologist Amy Cuddy studies body language and the impact it has on the mind. Her 2012 TED Talk, "Your Body Language May Shape Who You Are," suggests that our body language governs how we think and feel about ourselves, and thus, how we hold our bodies can have an impact on our minds. By taking a few minutes to stand in a power pose, you can alter your body's chemistry to make you feel more powerful. You'll know within one minute of doing this exactly what a power pose is. When we manage our emotional state well, it's much easier to usher in *elevated* emotions.

According to Dr. Joe Dispenza, an "elevated emotion" is a heart-centered emotion. They include love, compassion, gratitude, joy, unity, acceptance, inspiration, freedom, forgiveness, and kindness, to name a few. It reminds me of Nelson Mandela in the early 90s after he was unjustly imprisoned for twenty-seven years. Mandela forgave the people who took away all those years of his life. When asked how he survived those years, Mandela responded that he didn't *survive*, but instead, he *PREPARED*.

"Forgiveness liberates the soul," Mandela is often quoted saying. "Resentment is like drinking poison and hoping it will kill your enemies." He prepared to forgive so that if he did survive, he could let go and move on. "As I walked out the door toward the gate that would lead to my freedom," he said, "I knew that if I didn't leave my bitterness and hatred behind, I'd still be in prison."

I don't have words to do justice for that level of humanity in action. Mandela understood that forgiveness is not just a gift we give others, it is a gift we give ourselves. He chose elevated emotions. So can we. Your emotions are biochemical storms in your brain—and you are in control. We have the power to choose what emotions we want to feel.

The pitfall is defaulting to negative emotions like pain, suffering, and anger. We get addicted to these draining emotions, and breaking that addiction is exhausting and challenging, but it is a *must*. Use your body to counter that. Put your body into your affirmations, manage your emotional state, and choose elevated emotions. The rest will work itself out.

GRATITUDE JOURNAL

Another way in which to activate elevated emotions is by writing in a gratitude journal. Gratitude is the mother of all elevated emotions. It is a genuine and overwhelming gratefulness for life. There's a tremendous benefit to physically sitting down, picking up that pen, and writing in the journal. It doesn't take more than a few minutes. The benefits are outstanding; you can lower stress levels, and gain a greater sense of calmness and clarity. It reveals a fresh, positive perspective, which attracts more blessings.

Gratitude journaling is part of my nighttime routine. I reflect on the day and appreciate all the good that happened. Sometimes I just do it in my head, but writing is best. I've used a book called the *Five-Minute Journal*, which has morning and night prompts to record gratitude. I found the format helpful, but you don't have to buy a special book to do this. Take a regular journal or even pieces of paper and simply jot down what you are grateful for each day. It doesn't have to be fancy.

If you're someone who struggles with controlling your emotions or has a hard time choosing elevated ones, start with gratitude journaling. It gets a lot easier much faster than you think. Don't feel bad if when you start you can't think of much.

USING YOUR BODY CREATES ENERGY

When it comes to your goals, step one is to write them down, taking that thought in your head and transforming it from wishful thinking to something tangible. Next is to take that thought and turn it into a sound (frequency) by saying it out loud. By using our voices and creating sound, we are also using our bodies to elevate our emotional state and further contribute to creating energy. We have thus taken what started out as a mere thought and given it energy.

Using your body to put your goals, dreams, and aspirations out into the universe creates magnetism. By writing your goals down, repeating phrases over and over again, using your body to manage your emotional state, choosing elevated emotions, and expressing gratitude through journaling, you can create anything—wealth, love, health, and so on. These are the fundamentals, and fundamentals win championships.

When you put your voice and your body into your goals, you create energy and start to transform.

OUR HABITS BECOME OUR DESTINY

Destiny means "destination." We choose our habits, and our habits decide our destiny. Think about destiny like a GPS. You need to input the right address (habits) to arrive at the right destination (destiny). To be clear, I get it—life is hard, and this all sounds good on paper. There will be days that choosing happiness will feel out of reach, if not downright impossible. That's where the affirmations come in. I still have days that I choose lesser emotions. I fight my demons every day—most days I win, but *most* isn't all. The point is progress. I know my demons by their first names.

Use these tools to defy your negative programming.

Success is not linear. You're going to go through ups and downs. Expect it. By knowing this, you're more apt to conquer the challenge. If it were easy, everyone would do it. Trust the process. It works.

These challenges will appear countless times a day; it's a minute-to-minute battle. It's essential to turn these tools into concrete habits. You can't eat a salad for one meal and think you're suddenly the healthiest person in the world. You can't go to the gym one day and say you're ripped.

Jim Rohn says it best: "It's kind of like bathing; you can't just do it once." You must commit yourself to the practice. You must be consistent. Start by starting. Pick one tool. Nail it. Then incorporate another.

Baba was right: *Think & Grow Rich* was one of the most influential books I've ever read—and I'm constantly returning to it with a different perspective. Whenever I feel distracted or anxious, I'll flip to a random page. It's become a ritual for me—as if the universe is guiding me to the page that I need to read. Many of my most religious friends do this with their respective holy books and swear by its effectiveness. It's like that old saying from the Greek philosopher Heraclitus: "No man ever steps in the same river twice, for it's not the same river and he's not the same man."

This process will continue for the rest of my life because self-development is a never-ending pursuit. This pursuit would not be possible if I didn't take care of my health.

"Health is wealth," said Ralph Waldo Emerson. Tell me, what really matters if you don't have your health?

PART 2

LOOKING INWARD: BUILDING ON YOUR FOUNDATION

"Belief in oneself and knowing who you are, I mean, that's the foundation for everything great."
—JAY Z

CHAPTER 5

HEALTH IS WEALTH

"When health is absent, wisdom cannot reveal itself, art cannot manifest, strength cannot fight, wealth becomes useless, and intelligence cannot be applied."

—HEROPHILUS

In the early years of Rastegar, I took an amazing number of meetings. One was unforgettable: Dr. Jacob Rosenstein. His registered investment advisor, John Vann, decorated Vietnam veteran, published author and a Ph.D. in Economics, made the introduction. Dr. Vann and his son Aaron, both seasoned and brilliant, are partners in Vann Equity. Their risk management, ability to identify opportunity, and disciplined methodology still impress me.

Rosenstein has been a board-certified neurosurgeon and diplomate of the American Board of Neurological Surgery for almost four decades. Few are more accomplished, with over fourteen thousand successful operations under his care. In his early fifties at a family BBQ, David, his son, pointed out kindly but seriously that his health was not exactly *optimal.*

So, he set out on a quest to understand how and why we age. He grew curious to see whether aging was mandatory, whether it could be slowed, or possibly even be *optional*. Eventually, his proprietary system would revolutionize health and wellness. Some may call what he does *anti-aging* medicine. Not exactly.

At the end of the meeting, Rosenstein unexpectedly asked, "Can I say something that might sound personal?"

"Absolutely," I replied. "Anything."

"You look kind of tired. You have dark circles under your eyes. You're way too young for that."

He caught me off guard, especially after concluding a meticulous real estate discussion.

"Well...yeah," I admitted. "I'm exhausted."

"Your skin shows it. How do you sleep?" He asked in a gracious and endearing tone.

"Ha! What sleep? I'm running a business and raising a family. I'm lucky if I get a few solid hours."

"I'd like to take a look at your blood. I can help you." Rosenstein then shared how he, too, was overworked, lethargic, and unhealthy earlier in his life. Thirty years my senior, I sat across from a man in his sixties with 6 percent body fat, vibrant skin, and an energy about him that illuminated the room. Whatever he was doing was working. I was intrigued.

"Ari, your body is like an orchestra. You have flutes, cellos, violins, drums, and brass instruments, all playing their part. And I am the greatest conductor in the world." That is the only compliment I ever heard this gem of an individual say about himself.

His words resonated with me. We all know how one violin string left untuned can ruin an entire symphony. Similarly, one biochemical imbalance can set our bodies off course.

He continued his visual assessment of me: thinning hair, dark eye circles, cracked skin, and not much muscle mass. He was kind, honest, but very direct. He continued with detailed, probing questions about my mental, physical, and emotional health.

He dissected my health. I battled migraines, insomnia, and moments of anxiety. I learned these ailments directly correlated to diet, exercise, vitamins, and hormone imbalances. I had always been trim, but my body composition was worsening and my weight fluctuated. Simply, I didn't feel like myself.

My life was like an ongoing Olympic event; the demands of business were all consuming. I was running myself ragged. It took a toll in ways I didn't even understand. *Failure.*

"I'd love for you to draw my blood," I said. If there was a way to revitalize myself, I was all in. That decision changed my life, forever.

I eagerly submitted to the battery of tests, handing over twelve vials of blood for the most comprehensive medical exam I've ever taken. A full health analysis was an understatement. His program began with an executive health evaluation analyzing medical history, mental clarity, sexual health, risk factors, fitness, lifestyle, bone density, alignment, hormone levels, and heart health. He even tested my fitness level, grip strength, flexibility, balance, and cognitive function. With that and a slew of other data, he developed my personalized treatment plan.

The results revealed unusually low testosterone, high estrogen, high cholesterol, and vitamin deficiencies. I was also prediabetic and had several food allergies causing inflammation. I had two options. Option one: adopt the Mediterranean diet. Option two: go vegan. And in ninety days retest everything again.

I chose option two. I had a basic understanding of veganism. Rosenstein made certain I ate vegan the *right* way—meaning no simple carbs, processed sugar, or even certain fruits like bananas that are high in sugar. He emphasized sugar is the real killer of vitality, whether synthetic or natural. Modern-day diets are full of sugar in items you wouldn't expect—like bread, rice, and white potatoes. I was instructed to avoid those too.

I fully committed to plant protein, fruits, vegetables, and eliminating processed foods. I incorporated Rosenstein's exercise regimen and took daily supplements customized for me.

As entrepreneurs, optimal health is critical to long-term growth and productivity.

We all know that eating right and exercising is important; they are also deeply personal, so I will leave exploring what that looks like to you. Instead, this chapter is dedicated to the often overlooked aspects of healthy living: hydration, functional movement, posture management, breathing, and supplements.

HYDRATION

You might be thinking: *I know hydration is important.*

But do you, *really?*

I'm sure you know that our bodies are predominately water. Depending on the source, it ranges from 60 to 80 percent. Yes, water is crucial to keep the body functioning. Yes, it is present in our blood, skin, organs, and bones. Yes, there is water in every cell of the body, from the brain to the teeth.

There's so much more to proper hydration than we realize. For example, we've all heard the recommended "drink eight glasses of water a day" rule, but where did that arbitrary number even come from? It's just a simplified, one-size-fits-all way of trying to get people to drink water, regardless of their body composition, their activity level, or their age. Wrong! I believe a better method is to take your body weight in ounces divided by two. Start there.

Without consistent hydration, we're missing out on vast health benefits. According to one study done by Quench, most Americans (77 percent) admitted they don't drink enough water to meet their daily health needs.[3] Most acknowledge hydration is critical for our health, although we might not understand how bad dehydration is for our bodies. Common ailments attributed to dehydration include fatigue, dizziness, dry skin, muscle cramps, mood swings, headaches—and bad breath! Even mild dehydration can have a negative impact on productivity, energy levels, and alertness. Oftentimes what we perceive as hunger is really dehydration in disguise. Drink more water! The old scientific cliché is "Pollution dilution."

You have toxins in your body—we all do—dilute them and flush them out with water. Not just any liquid. *Water!*

To take it a step further, drinking enough water is great, but you need to have the proper mineral electrolyte balance, too. Our cells are bathed in mineral-rich fluids that help regulate the transport of nutrients and waste products to and from every tissue and organ. Not hydrating properly, layered with our lifestyle choices and high-stress lives, deplete those minerals, disrupting and compromising our cellular function. It's essential to not only drink water, but the right type of water with electrolytes.

You can find companies that offer sugar-free electrolyte supplements online. I use Tom Brady's brand frequently. One of their products offered on the TB12 website is their highly-reviewed electrolyte supplement—which is both inexpensive and highly effective. Or go on Amazon, read the reviews, and consider purchasing an electrolyte liquid supplement to add to your water. I find this to be an overlooked element to achieving peak performance—and it's surprisingly affordable. Remember to read the ingredients, and if possible, choose only sugar-free products for obvious reasons.

When at home, I use a seawater liquid mineral supplement called Quinton. It's a purified seawater extract that contains up to seventy-eight minerals. These liquid mineral supplements are harvested from raw, nutrient-rich marine fluid from protected plankton blooms off the coast of France. I know what you're thinking: *You drink seawater? Gross!*

Seawater, the purest form of natural electrolytes, is a gentle daily supplement that impacts everything—from cellular, brain, and immune system functionality. It's not like I drink seawater all day long. Just one small ampule of Quinton or TB12's equivalent has resounding benefits.

If you take your hydration seriously, then I recommend drinking some form of purified water. I prefer alkaline water and use a filter at home. There is a wide variety of excellent brands that you can find online at a reasonable price. I think Brita has earned a solid reputation. I stay away from unfiltered tap water and most store-bought bottles due to a high concentration of toxins. Once your water is cleansed of contaminants, it becomes a better delivery vehicle for the nutrients your body requires.

It is important to move your body when you drink water. Movement gets water into your cells. This could be as simple as going for a short walk. When you consume water while incorporating movement, the water travels more effectively through your system.

Although I won't tell you what diet you should subscribe to, it's important to remember so much of hydration comes from food. As such, pick a diet that is full of water-based foods. Regardless of what diet works for you, eat green leafy vegetables and fruits because they will hydrate you in addition to providing essential vitamins, fiber, and antioxidants. If you eat a lot of processed foods, you're probably not getting enough water.

Going vegan for a year helped lower my cholesterol in part because I started eating more vegetables, which helped hydrate my body and enable it to improve. I no longer strictly practice veganism, although many swear by it. For my own nutrition, I've found my body responds best to a plant-based, predominately vegetarian diet mixed with small amounts of fresh wild fish and some organic chicken. Before going vegan, I thought I drank enough water. I didn't.

FUNCTIONAL MOVEMENT

When was the last time you put your arms over your head?

That might be a strange question, but I'm referring to how our modern-day lifestyles aren't conducive to using the body the way it was intended. Functional movement is about moving the way we used to as hunters and gatherers—crawling under bushes, climbing trees, jumping over streams and boulders, etc.

Functional movements are archetypal movements, like squats, putting your arms over your head, bear crawling, crab walking, and so on. These movements you don't typically do in everyday life, but when you do, you're engaging more muscles and reducing atrophy. An easy way to visualize this is to watch children at play. They do almost all of this innately—and all while having a blast!

The saying is true: If you don't use it, you lose it.

We don't put our arms over our heads anymore because most of us don't have a daily need for climbing. Predominately, we sit at a desk in front of a computer or on our phones, which causes a lot of tension in our necks and upper spine. This, in turn, affects the way we feel and function. As a society, we have developed "tech neck," where we strain our neck forward because we spend so much time looking at our devices. When you put your hands over your head, you open up your chest and lungs. Remember when you choked as a kid and an adult would tell you to put your hands over your head? It's because doing so opens your airways. That's what we want. So put your hands over your head, swing on monkey bars, climb trees, and jump around, because they all open your lungs. Embrace your inner child.

If you look at dopamine and serotonin production, science has proven jumping or bouncing to be a highly effective way to stimulate brain function. Jumping rope, jumping on trampolines, running, and jumping over obstacles stimulate healthy fundamental chemicals in your brain. As we get older, we don't jump as much, if at all. As you jump less, your functionality also lessens. As such, I have a small trampoline in my office that I use from time to time throughout the day.

POSTURE MANAGEMENT

Posture is the position in which we hold our bodies while standing, sitting, or lying down. Improper posture negatively affects our health and wellbeing, and in turn, our productivity.

I subscribe mostly to the posture management modality of Egoscue, which is a customized protocol of functional movement exercises to help fix alignment issues. It was founded by Pete Egoscue, who wrote a book called *Pain Free* and a series of other books, all worth reading, and more importantly, implementing.

I saw a presentation about the Egoscue Method, where the science behind the philosophy and techniques was explained. The presenters stated how important proper posture is for our cerebral spinal fluid to travel to our brains. They talked about how poor posture leads to injuries, pain, and permanent damage if left unaddressed. For instance, it doesn't matter how good your diet is if you're slouched over and crushing your intestines; your intestines aren't going to work the way they're designed to!

Over the years, I noticed my gait had changed and, as a result, I was slouched and frequently uncomfortable or in pain. In my pursuit of peak performance, I read Pete's book and found in Austin, Texas, a local practitioner, Rick Mathes, who is now a dear friend. After analyzing pictures of my body's condition at the time, Rick prescribed a series of exercises he called my custom "menu." These movements targeted muscles that were overcompensating in an effort to calm down the muscles that were overworked and to reactivate atrophied muscles, all to regain proper body posture and balance. After one session, my gait improved, and I walked more upright. Over the next several months, my pain had all but vanished, and I had regained strength in areas I had not anticipated.

At Rastegar, as a firm, we value health and wellness. There's a gym right next to my office, so I do those exercises in some capacity every day. You would be surprised to see how much of this I am able to do in my office throughout the day during short interval breaks from sitting at my desk or talking on the phone.

You don't have to do Egoscue or anything fancy to get the benefits of an active body and a sharp mind. Here's the bottom line: Sitting is the new smoking, so stand up and do some light stretches every day. If you can't make it to the gym or do posture management exercises, get up and walk around while on the phone. Simple movements during the day maintain your health and wellbeing more than you may know.

PROPER BREATHING

If you look at the hierarchy of importance to health, the most important is oxygen. If you don't breathe for three to five minutes, you die. The next one is water. If you don't drink water for seven days, give or take, you die. Then food. If you don't eat for approximately sixty days, you die. So, focus on those in that order.

Studies show that we can equate breathing to just about every emotion. We breathe a certain way when we're happy, when we're sad, when we're angry. By learning to breathe properly, we invigorate the cells in our body, which is essential since our whole body is governed by oxygen. Unfortunately, most of us have poor breathing patterns because we've never been taught how to breathe skillfully—and that's exactly what it is: a skill.

Abdominal breathing, where you breathe through your nose (your mouth is for laughing and eating) is considered proper breathing—and it's also the most overlooked component of good health. Breathing is necessary for life, but what many of us don't consider is that breathing is also the quickest, easiest, and most rewarding solution to deal with stress, depression, fatigue, and anxiety. Learning how to breathe properly is worth it.

The benefits of effective breathing techniques have been emphasized by most ancient cultures, but these days the most discussed technique is rooted in yoga, called pranayama. Pranayama is the formal practice of controlling the breath, which is the source of our prana, or vital life force, as avid yogis believe. In pranayama practice, you learn to activate your breath to invigorate the body, which sometimes results in a tingly feeling in the face, hands, and legs. There are numerous breathing techniques, each of which purports to lower your resting heart rate, which allows your body to heal. Unfortunately, it's a skill we're not taught in conventional schooling systems.

Although I've done some variation of pranayama in conjunction with my meditation, I wasn't necessarily consistent about it. When Wim Hof—also known as "the Iceman," a nickname he earned after running a half-marathon barefoot in the Arctic Circle—started appearing in the media a few years back, he brought a lot of attention to the importance of breathing mechanics. This got me thinking about breathing again too. I'm focused now more than ever on improving my breathing skills, and you should be too. Wim has a free App that is highly beneficial to get you started.

SUPPLEMENTS

Following IBISWorld data, at the end of 2021, the dietary supplement industry was worth $35.7 billion in the United States.[4] As such, supplements are a bit of a rabbit hole. To make it easier and actionable, I want to focus on the one thing that helps all: a high-quality multivitamin.

In general, modern humans are systemically deficient in vitamin D, and a slew of other basic elements. I'm a fan of Pure Encapsulations as a brand, but do your research and check with your doctor before adding any supplements to your diet. I thought I was on the right path with my supplements, but Rosenstein taught me that not every supplement is created equally.

When I first saw Rosenstein, he put me on various vitamins to balance my deficiencies. I've always taken vitamins, so this was nothing new to me. In fact, my wife and kids often make fun of me because I can swallow thirty pills at once without a problem.

What was new was the quality of vitamins I began to take. Rosenstein explained how a lot of the supplements out there significantly underdeliver what their marketing touts. I have since switched all my supplements to ones he recommended. His brand, VitaYears, makes the best multivitamin, in my opinion. My family and closest friends take them and have experienced similar positive results. There are many great ones out there; do your research, read the ingredients, but most importantly, take them!

A BETTER ME

"It is health that is real wealth and not pieces of gold and silver."

—MAHATMA GANDHI

I admire Steve Jobs' contributions to the world; he admitted on numerous occasions, though, that he got one thing wrong: not valuing his health. He expressed that he grew too obsessed with business at the expense of his family life and his health. His loss, his family's loss, the world's loss, was nothing short of tragic. He had so much more to give. His death still haunts me and serves as reminder to do whatever is in my control to take care of myself as best I can. Rest in peace, Steve. You are dearly missed.

Improving my health caused everything else in my life to improve. I even think I became a better person. My relationship with my kids and family improved since I had more energy to give them the best of me, not the leftovers, and was able to be more present.

I certainly became a better businessman, and the results were obvious. The long hours weren't as draining or irritable. I ate and slept better. My cognitive abilities were sharper and more in focus, allowing me to make even better decisions. The more I worked on increasing hydration, improving my posture, and taking high-quality supplements, the better I performed. Everything correlated directly to my bottom line. The bottom line was me. I was better.

I'll be doing this for the rest of my life, which I expect to be long and full of vitality and contribution. I seek to constantly improve my process and stay curious about advances in science to tweak my regimen. As time has gone on, I've added different exercises, added new supplements, and advanced my breathing techniques. I'm always looking to see if there's more I can do—more that I can give. I'm quite literally obsessed with growth and contribution.

For example, I used to meditate twice a day for twenty minutes. Now I meditate forty-five minutes a day twice a day, and when I can, I do it in a hyperbaric chamber, which has resounding health benefits by itself. I'm exploring infrared light beds and IV therapies, different vitamins, trampolines, and brain training techniques. Before, I didn't have the energy to explore these things. Now I double-down on what matters most.

CHAPTER 6

YOU ARE YOUR BRAND

"Dressing well is a form of good manners."

—TOM FORD

People say we shouldn't judge a book by its cover. But let's be real, we all do. First impressions matter. It's high priority to nail your personal presentation, because a person's initial assessment of you can last a long time, if not forever.

My parents have always dressed impeccably well. My father, after becoming an attorney, routinely wore Giorgio Armani suits and Bally shoes, which he saw as an investment. My mom always had an innate sense of style and elegance. She had an eye for fashion, even when we shopped at yard sales and thrift stores. It shows you that style has nothing to do with money. She taught me that.

I savored sweats most of my life, and I would be remiss not to say that I still love my lululemon, not to mention my closet full of Walmart's finest jogging suits that I keep on hand for my meditation retreats. These days, if I'm not in a suit (which is more often than I would like), I'm in our custom Rastegar gear. Hats, shoes, hoodies, masks, robes, you name it, we brand it. You can be sure it's high quality, but affordable. It's the Rastegar way.

How you carry yourself matters. Dressing well changes your state of mind, how you move, your stride, and your confidence. Pay attention to your appearance. Observe those you aspire to emulate not only in their results but in how they carry themselves and how they appear in public. Just like anything else, you can learn the art of personal style. In hindsight, it took me longer than I would have liked before recognizing how necessary this is. My failure to realize this sooner led to a lot of bad first impressions—translated, potential missed opportunities.

Straight out of law school I got a job working in New York City. I knew I had to immediately add some nice suits to my wardrobe. So, I went shopping. The high-price-tag suits that I wanted were out of reach, but I did what I could with my measly budget, picking out the best-looking suit and pair of shoes I could afford.

The suit didn't fit well. It was too large around the waist and shoulders, making me look awkward. I didn't feel my best, but I sucked it up. At least it was clean. *This is as good as it's going to get for now*, I told myself.

In Manhattan, arguably one of the world's fashion epicenters, I was surrounded by people who dressed to the nines, which made me feel inferior. I was so lucky to work with legendary business magnates. These individuals dominated any room they walked in, like shiny objects stealing your attention. They would invite me to join them for dinners and business meetings, and all looked sharp, even in casual attire. They knew the secret, and it wasn't frills. It was classy, clean, well-fitting, and understated elegance.

Some made small digs about my look: "When you grow up, Ari," they said teasing me, "you'll get a nice suit that actually fits you." Although these comments weren't meant to be mean spirited—just poking a little fun at the rookie—it still hurt a little.

I was embarrassed because they were right.

Although I couldn't afford a $3,000 custom tailored suit at the time, I took what I had and found a tailor who could at least minimize the bagginess for one hundred dollars. It helped dramatically. A great tailor can make a cheap suit appear infinitely better—they are the last of a dying breed of true artists. That said, even the best artist is limited by their materials. Adjusting my frumpy suit was a temporary solution. Internally, I groaned at work, knowing I could do better. I set a goal for myself: to save enough money to afford a proper suit.

In typical Ari fashion, I didn't just want *any* tailored suit. I wanted a suit from Martin Greenfield, one of the most famous custom tailors in the world.

He wrote a fascinating memoir called *Measure of a Man: From Auschwitz Survivor to Presidents' Tailor*. As the legend goes, Mr. Greenfield has tailored a custom suit for every president since Eisenhower. He's been called "America's greatest living tailor" and "the most interesting man in the world," so I set my heart on having my very own *Martin Greenfield*. It took about a year and a half of working and saving, but I was finally ready to step up my game. I called Mr. Greenfield's shop in Brooklyn and made an appointment. I was ecstatic. They scheduled me with one of his students, Stevie, or better known as "Stevie the Tailor." He made me my first true *custom* suit, but it would not be ready for six weeks. *Six weeks?!* I was so ready for that suit. I had endured the frumpiness, the comments, and the embarrassment for long enough, and here I had to endure it for six more weeks?

It was a long six weeks.

It was a special day when I was called back to try it on for the first time. I felt so proud. I looked at Stevie and saw the sparkle in his eye too. I'll never forget it. Deep down I still wanted an original Martin Greenfield and planned to have the legend himself make me one when it was my time, but I was happy to wait. To my dismay and deep sadness, not long after my fitting, Stevie was involved in a tragic accident on a four-wheeler, protecting his daughter from harm. Thankfully, he survived. I still think of Stevie and his family every time I put on that suit.

My wardrobe of suits quickly doubled in size from one to two. But I needed another suit to add to my small collection, so I went back to Mr. Greenfield's shop. I had a chance run-in with Mr. Greenfield himself.

"You're Stevie's friend, right?" he said.

"Yes," I said softly, still feeling a bit uncomfortable.

He replied, "Stand over here," pointing to the box step up to start my fitting. I thought to myself, *It's happening.*

After he finished my measurements, his son Jay, now a friend, took my credit card. It was a dream come true.

I dropped everything when I got the call that it was ready for pick-up and immediately headed to 239 Varet Street in Brooklyn, where his shop has been for over half a century. When I tried on the gray three-piece suit, I couldn't believe my eyes.

What a transformation! It was surreal. *That* man in the mirror is who I wanted to be. I felt like a more capable person. There are no words to describe the feeling. Anything felt possible.

In that suit, I felt a shift. Instead of embarrassment, I was filled with confidence. It was a ton of money for me at the time, but worth every penny. For my birthday, my wife (then girlfriend) completed the look, gifting me a pair of Louis Vuitton dress shoes. I still have and wear them to this day.

I felt like a billion bucks! The first time I wore my new suit to work, I met with a colleague who immediately noticed. "Damn, Ari. You look fantastic!" he said.

"What do you mean?" I said, pretending I didn't know what he was referring to.

"What did you do different? You look like a new man."

No teasing this time about ill-fitting suits, although there were new jokes like: This guy spends all his money on suits! Learn to embrace the jokes; it's just back-handed jealousy mixed with admiration. Smile and nod. Dress for the job you want. The investment in the suits was worth it—and I realized that it truly was an *investment*—not an expense or an exercise in vanity. I assure you, it paid generous dividends. I've continued to invest in quality apparel. I take appearance seriously, and so should you. People notice and will treat you accordingly.

> Clothes are an investment, not an expense, and the dividends they pay are immeasurable. We always judge a book by its cover—and for a while, I wore a boring, ill-fitting cover. *Failure!*

YOU ARE A BRAND

"Clothes make the man. Naked people have little or no influence on society."

—MARK TWAIN

There's a ton of talk about branding companies, but what about branding *yourself?*

Starbucks sells coffee and Microsoft sells software; you sell something too—*you.* This includes your personality, work ethic, character, and aspirations—all of which are influential. You are your own public relations, sales, and marketing departments all rolled into one. When you position your image in a favorable light, you automatically remove natural, society-created barriers that will aid your career and life.

According to the Carnegie Institute of Technology, 85 percent of your financial success is due to skills in "human engineering," like your personality and ability to communicate.[5] When I say you are your own brand, I'm talking about characteristics noticeable from the get-go. Eighty percent of communication is nonverbal. People notice and judge what you're wearing, how you carry yourself, how well-groomed you are, and so on. If you don't care for your appearance, people will make negative judgments.

Dressing well helped build my business because clients took me more seriously. You don't have to go overboard. In fact, you shouldn't. You don't need an entire wardrobe full of expensive clothes, just some select items that you wear strategically. Remember, it is not the cost per se. I've seen plenty of expensive garments that look cheap and sloppy, just as I've seen plenty of cheap clothing worn well. Dressing appropriately is as much an art as it is a science.

It's not about how much you spend; it's about presentation. I owned a few suits for the first three years of my career—a dark blue, gray, and black suit—but few would notice because I rotated other elements to keep things fresh. I'd switch up my shoes, ties, and shirts: white and blue shirts, solid ties. No frills, no handkerchief, no watch, no cufflinks. Clean and elegant.

Get a couple of different white and/or blue shirts and some ties from Nordstrom Rack or Neiman Marcus LastCall. You can also buy gently used designer shirts and ties on sites like eBay or Poshmark. Be thrifty. You can find quality clothes for a great price and then take them to a tailor. There's nothing quite like clothing specifically fitted for your body.

Dressing well increases performance and self-esteem. When wearing something that fits you beautifully, you feel good, and you act as such in all respects. You carry yourself better—and people notice it. This applies to children, too. If you give a five-year-old a pair of their favorite shoes, they are going to feel better about themselves both internally and socially. This might sound old-school, but shine your shoes, or at least keep them very clean. For many years, I shined my shoes every day, even though the shoes I had weren't the best quality.

DON'T BE FLASHY

"Elegance is not about being noticed. It's about being remembered."

—GIORGIO ARMANI

What you wear is an easy way to change your mentality. Why do I wear lululemon? It's not only super comfortable; it looks good, and you can wash them a hundred times and they still look like new. Great brand, great value.

Spend the extra money on a professional haircut and take care of your fingernails because people will notice those too. Your hands and your head are always exposed. You can tell a lot about a pair of hands. I used to bite my nails, so I started getting manicures to prevent me from biting. Since that is a luxury, which it was for me, I learned to do it myself. So can you.

A lot of your outward appearance will come from how you take care of your internal health. Hydrate for better skin, eat well for energy and vitality, and exercise. What does a preventable, poor appearance tell a colleague or potential client? It could imply you don't take care of yourself, which could mean you don't respect yourself. In my opinion, if you don't respect yourself, why should your clients believe you'll respect them?

When you take care of yourself, it is much easier to access those elevated emotions. All of this leads to you being an all-around better person.

When it comes to your brand, aim for understated elegance. You don't want the attention to go to what you're wearing; you want the attention to go to *you*. Don't be flashy; that exudes arrogance, and no one likes that. Be humble, but confident. In fact, some of the most powerful people I know are the humblest. Humility is not thinking less of yourself.

You also need to know your audience and dress accordingly. I work in a lot of construction zones, so I don't wear my expensive suits out in the field. If I wore a suit to a construction site, people would think I'm pretentious—not to mention a total idiot. I don't want to ruin my suit at a dirty construction site, either. I'll wear something more practical. If I'm meeting with a banker, on the other hand, well, that's a different story. I'll be busting out my finest wear to be on brand, although I might skip the tie in the Texas summer. Know your audience as well as you know yourself, or even better. The point is, when you brand yourself properly, people will want to do business with you.

INVESTING VS. SPENDING

I'm always looking for deep value. It is who I am and what I do. When you invest, you're seeking to create value. Spending, on the other hand, is the opposite: wasting money on things that don't add value.

Investing in you encompasses many different practices. Some examples include self-help books, online courses to learn a new skill, and a gym membership (or go online and do virtual free classes with the best trainers in the world). Spending money, by contrast, would include things like frivolously dining out, daily coffee at your local java joint, and unnecessary vanity. Seek value, not ego or vanity. After all, this is business.

The same thought goes for developing proper hygiene. This isn't just good for your brand, it's good for your health. For instance, poor dental hygiene is the leading cause of heart disease. If it's a part of your brand, it's worth focusing on and improving. Ensure you're presenting your best self. Dressing well and keeping up with your hygiene is a sign of self-respect—which I believe, ultimately, tells your clients how much you respect them.

If you had a meeting with someone who was pitching to manage your family's finances and they were unkempt and had dirty clothes, what immediate impression would you have of them? If they don't care for themselves, how can you expect them to take care of you and your family? Conversely, if you met with someone who was well groomed, healthy looking, in clean clothes, you would subconsciously or consciously note that this individual takes care of themselves, so you can more likely trust that they would do the same for you. If that's how they treat themselves, imagine how they are going to treat you.

No one will really respect you if you don't respect your-self. Your personal image—your brand—has a huge impact on the way people judge you.

A POWERFUL TOOL

"You can have anything you want in life, if you dress for it."

—EDITH HEAD

What you wear and your outward appearance is a powerful tool to master. Do not underestimate its significance. You can make yourself more assertive based on your clothes and personal hygiene alone. Invest in yourself to leave a good impression with others and see where it can take you.

I'm personally a strong believer in the notion that taking care of yourself and wearing fashionable clothes can make you more charismatic and likable, which is a key ingredient in building relationships. When you brand yourself so that people are attracted to you, they'll want to do business with you, which is what we'll cover in the next chapter.

CHAPTER 7

RELATIONSHIPS
RULE THE WORLD

"If you believe business is built on relationships, make building them your business."

—SCOTT STRATTEN

Relationships have always been important to me, but that doesn't mean I always had the right approach or understood just how paramount they really are in every facet of life. When I first started Rastegar, I was temporarily wrapped up in trying to get in front of people to ask them to partner with us on deals. I was told that it was a numbers game. If I got in front of enough people, a handful of them were bound to join me. It turns out that wasn't exactly right.

I can be a relatively outgoing and chatty guy, especially after seven years of speech therapy, which helped build the skills I needed to communicate more effectively. Over time, I became close with a lot of people from varying backgrounds and industries, who graciously introduced me to their networks. One of those was a junior associate at a financial firm who worked for several well-established money managers I only knew by reputation. I was lucky enough to get a warm introduction.

One Saturday afternoon, we met at the manager's country club. "I've heard a lot about you," he told me as we situated ourselves for lunch. "Tell me more about yourself."

I started to talk about Rastegar, the goals of the company, our risk management process, and thesis. In short, I was pitching a series of projects. Business, all business.

"No, no, Ari," I was stopped abruptly. "We'll get to your company. I want to get to know *you*."

Oh. I proceeded to narrate my life story: where I grew up, that I'm an attorney by trade, my failed Capital A adventure, meeting my wife, my kids, my love of French fries, and so on. There was no discussion about the company for the rest of our meeting.

"Let's do lunch again next week, and bring your dad."

Bring my dad? I thought the request was strange, but I went with it. As requested, my dad joined us for lunch the following week. Just like the week prior, there was no talk of business. We remained in frequent contact throughout that year. We shared some laughs as we got to know each other. All the questions felt intrusive, but respectful. Sometimes, I would get a call out of the blue to ask where I was. "In my office, where I always am. Why? Where are *you*?"

"I'm coming by right now," he said.

Although it might sound intense, in hindsight, it was genuine interest and due diligence. Those encounters were the building blocks that created mutual trust. In building any meaningful new relationship, I'm reminded of the truth in President Ronald Reagan's words, "Trust, but verify." Before people begin learning about your business, they will want to get to know *you* to get comfortable with who you are and what you stand for. *Then* they'll want to know about your business. This trust is cultivated and nurtured historically through tribal moments such as sharing meals and meeting each other's friends and family. This all combines to create what we call an *authentic relationship*. It does not happen overnight, and it shouldn't, if it is built to last.

I have been very fortunate that many of my encounters like this have lasted the test of time and have been mutually beneficial and greatly rewarding. Do not be discouraged if certain relationships never flourish; it's good to know that sooner than later.

Early on, I immediately led with data, rarely taking the time to build a relationship. I will never know how many deals I lost by ignoring the intangibles and getting lost in the facts. *Failure.*

AUTHENTIC RELATIONSHIPS ARE EVERYTHING

"Succeeding in business is all about making connections."

—RICHARD BRANSON

Whatever "success" I have had is unequivocally due to relationships—even dating back to the Capital A days. One of the gifts from that failure was the many relationships I'd established and maintained. Relationships are fragile and need to be nurtured. They require care and attention. People are not stupid, and you can't fake authenticity. This requires dedicated time and effort. Done properly and led with heart, the byproduct reaps immeasurable rewards.

In the early years, my feelings would get hurt when people did not take me seriously. By putting my ego aside, I came to accept that I was the rookie on the block. By real estate standards, I was quite young to be doing what I was doing at an institutional level, so I understood the healthy skepticism.

People were just doing their job getting to know me or choosing not to. I always respect people that do their jobs in good faith. I had to let the results of my efforts speak for themselves. That was going to take time. And time it took, but it all changed as we continued to grow, achieve, and serve consistently.

These days, I'm grateful for those times. I learned resilience and a commitment to refine what wasn't working. It was a good reminder to cherish the relationships I had and to spend time deepening them, all the while building new ones. These relationships and the humanity that comes with cultivating them taught me so much. Many of the prospective clients who initially said no, eventually said yes.

RELATIONSHIP BUILDING 101

"Slow down and make building relationships as important as building projects."

—GREG MORTENSON

As problem solvers, many entrepreneurs are great at developing solutions, but then struggle to make them into a business because they don't realize that running a business requires relationships. You need to build relationships with a wide range of people: project partners, peers, vendors, public officials, consultants, employees, and of course, customers.

This harkens back to how business has nothing to do with business, and how you are your biggest asset. It's about who you are as a person, and how you treat those around you. A lot of success in business boils down to whether you're likable: people work with people they like. If they like you, they'll find a way to do business with you.

Warren Buffet once said, "It takes twenty years to build a reputation and five minutes to ruin it. If you think about that, you'll do things differently." I've thought about this quote a lot over the years, and it's helped shape how I approach building and maintaining relationships—business and personal. The following represent some of the ways in which I prioritize this.

THE POWER OF NETWORKING

Since relationships rule the world, you should do everything you can to get in front of as many of the *right* people. Put yourself out there; you never know who you might meet.

We're all familiar with networking opportunities—like conferences, happy hours, meetups, seminars, trade shows, luncheons, and roundtable discussions—but networking doesn't have to be this formal. You can strike up a friendly conversation with someone just about anywhere. As long as you are engaging with other people, you are networking. Social media has made this easier than ever. There are no good excuses not to connect and build relationships.

Some might cringe at the thought of this, but don't neglect the power of cold calling. I literally built Rastegar on cold calling vendors, consultants, or anyone that could help me. I would often just show up at the office of the person I wanted to meet. I made friends with people from all walks of life. It's amazing what being pleasant and some cookies can do to jump-start a relationship. Were some people annoyed? Sure, but not everyone. You don't need to win them all.

I love cold calling offices and getting people to chat with me. Since cold calling isn't as popular as it used to be, I found that it leaves a better impression than cold emailing. Emails are all too easy to ignore or go into the spam folder. Dynamic and positive things happen when you simply speak to people. Pick whatever method is best suited to you and your business. I always prefer to meet in person. We are tribal beings; in person, we connect on a deeper and more authentic level.

Do not be afraid of going old school—with cold calling, but also with snail mail, taking clients out to dinner, meeting family members, and so on—because old-school still works. Although technology is amazing and it has elevated all aspects of our lives, there's something special about being a human wanting to connect with another human.

KEEP THINGS SIMPLE

"Everything should be made as simple as possible, but not simpler."

—ALBERT EINSTEIN

One of my mentors, Doug Herman, an extremely successful businessman, gave me some advice that stuck: "When you're going to explain an idea to someone, you need to make it as simple as possible." In other words, he said you need to tell the story in such a way that whoever you're talking to can go home and tell their significant other or their advisors the same story without losing its clarity and simplicity. Complexity is the enemy of execution.

Even if your product or service is highly technical, you need to prioritize ways you can explain it simply and understandably without losing the power of the message. No one likes feeling stupid, and when they do, that's an impression that is not easy to undo.

BUILD TRUST

The key to building trust is being brutally honest. Nothing is guaranteed, especially in my line of work. Things out of our control can happen at any time—and often when you least expect. Once trust is established, even if things go wrong (which they will), your clients will trust that you will protect their interests. This is the power of real, deep, long-lasting relationships. Trust doesn't come right away, nor should it; it is built over time, brick by brick.

BE AUTHENTIC

This is pretty simple. Be who you are and accept others as they are. As American professor and author Brené Brown once said, "Authenticity is a collection of choices that we have to make every day. It's about the choice to show up and be real. The choice to be honest. The choice to let our true selves be seen." Hiding or suppressing who we really are warps our communication and damages our relationships, perhaps not immediately, but inevitably.

Don't try to be someone you are not; people can feel it, and no one responds well to those who aren't real. Authenticity requires vulnerability, transparency, and integrity. Accept the fact that you aren't for everyone, nor are your products. The good news is, if your product or service is valuable, there are customers waiting. You just need to find them, and eventually they will find you.

For many of us, communication doesn't come naturally. In fact, some surveys have even shown that many people are more afraid of public speaking than they are of death. Even Warren Buffett—one of the wealthiest, most successful people in history—had an acute fear of speaking until he actively took steps to overcome it. He once confessed, "My public speaking course was arguably the best investment I made in my life."

When it comes to communication, fear is not an excuse for

inaction. Communication is key in any relationship, especially your business ones. When you communicate effectively and consistently with your colleagues, your employees, and your clients, you build and earn their trust. If you want to learn a new skill, do what Warren Buffet did and learn the art of communication.

In any business, transparent communication must be a cornerstone core value. Keep your clients in the loop on everything relevant, and I urge an open-door policy. When in doubt, over-communicate.

CONNECTION IS KEY

"Business, after all, is nothing more than a bunch of human relationships."

—LEE IACOCCA

I've been fortunate to have always valued relationships, not knowingly, but inherently. This is evident in still maintaining close contact with Coach and Anthony. I certainly learned a lot from them. When I look backward, I can see how all the dots connected. Capital A didn't work out as planned, but twelve years and counting after our stint in the entertainment industry "failed," we're still doing deals together. A failure turned into success. We aren't just friends anymore. We are family.

That relationship was the source of many more deep relationships, such as one of my most precious relationships with Jeff DiModica, the President of Starwood Capital, who has always been a wise sounding board, trustworthy, and full of wisdom. I always learn something when I'm around him. His guidance has helped me navigate some tough obstacles, and I will be forever grateful. In the end, all of these seeming failures have led to something far more valuable than how they originated. I am in awe of how the blessings have unfolded and continue to expand.

You never know who is going to impact your life now, or in the future. You must have faith that it will lead you where you are meant to be.

Next, we'll transcend beyond the mental and physical. We'll start with dismantling the all-too-common but flawed idea of work-life balance.

PART 3

TRANSCENDING BEYOND THE PHYSICAL

"If constructive thoughts are planted, positive
outcomes will be the result. Plant the seeds
of failure and failure will follow."
—SIDNEY MADWED

CHAPTER 8

THERE'S NO SUCH THING AS WORK-LIFE BALANCE

"Focus like a laser, not a flashlight."

—MICHAEL JORDAN

In college, I had too many ideas and not enough action. I was told I had attention deficit disorder (ADD) and that I was all over the place. I wanted to dip my fingers in *everything.* They called it ADD, but I saw it as ADA: attention deficit *advantage.* I had a lot to do—and I learned that you can do it all—just not today. So, I lasered in.

I was an attorney by trade.

I wanted to write a great American novel and take it to Hollywood.

I wanted to do real estate.

I wanted to build a revolutionary technology company.

I even wanted to venture into fashion at one point (don't ask).

Maybe politics—why not?

I wanted it all, but nothing was working effectively because I was just dabbling. It wasn't until I homed in on one idea, Rastegar, that I finally saw success. The sunlight finally hit the magnifying glass at just the right angle and the business caught fire.

> I was once a Jack of all trades, but a master of none, as the saying goes. I didn't give any one idea the laser focus it needed, so nothing took off. *Failure.*

I don't want to limit your dreams because you *can* do everything in life, *just not all at once.* Focus on one thing and become great at that one thing first. Once you've mastered it and become an expert, you can figure out how to automate it, delegate it, and operate it from afar. Then move on to the next thing. Conquer, and then proceed to the next goal.

There's no such thing as work-life balance—not if you want mind-blowing, astronomical success. Work-life balance is a fantasy. To that effect, multitasking is a lie, too. It dilutes energy. Multitasking is like setting off on a road trip without deciding on a route and stopping to get directions every few minutes. You lose momentum and waste time.

Work-life balance and multitasking don't exist for those of us who are visionaries chasing the wildest of dreams. They're just propaganda—a couple of fun buzz phrases to toss around for the average consumer to work toward. Hey, if that's something they want, then they can go for it—I'm not trying to dismiss the idea, but it's not for people like you and me. We want more.

That's why we have to implement a seesaw mentality.

BECOME A SEESAW

Instead of pursuing this elusive *balance*, you must teeter like a seesaw between the two extremes of work and home to be wildly successful. Seesawing means you're 100 percent focused on what's in front of you. When you're at work, be 100 percent at work; when you're at home, be 100 percent at home. You must learn how to be fully present and seesaw fully from one activity to another in whatever you're doing.

> Seesawing is about greatness, excellence, focus, and most of all, being unequivocally present for the task at hand.

When I say you are 100 percent focused on the thing in front of you, I mean an all-encompassing, excessive focus. You must be all-in. Your focus needs to be like a spotlight, not a floodlight. It could be a phone call, an email, a workout, dinner, or helping your kid with homework. Whatever it is, you give it your full and undivided attention. Be 100 percent obsessively *all in*.

Let's say you're doing pushups. When you get into the high plank position to start your set, you seesaw all your focus and energy to prepare to descend. Your mind is focused on where your hands are, on engaging your core for support, and on your breathing. When you make your descent to the ground, you're taking note of your form so that you're not arching your back while keeping your quads engaged. All your focus is on making sure each pushup is as perfect as possible. During your set, you shut your brain off from thinking about anything else and solely concentrate on making one flawless pushup at a time, one by one, until you finish your set.

Shut out the noise. It's a skill that must be cultivated. Work on it and master it. It is like a muscle. You must work at it over and over until it becomes a rock-solid habit. Seesawing is a philosophy and a skill. It's a way of life. You must integrate it into everything you do.

To successfully seesaw back and forth, make sure you're good with the foundational principles we previously laid out. Be sturdy. After all, who would trust their kids on a wobbly, loose-screwed seesaw?

Your health needs to be a priority for you to have the gas in the tank to give 100 percent to your family after an arduous day of work. You need to be exercising, hydrating, and meditating so that you can successfully seesaw back and forth. When you take care of yourself and treat yourself like an asset, seesawing will be easier to practice.

IT'S NOT EASY, AND DON'T EXPECT IT TO BE

Seesawing to the extreme is not normal. *Everything worth doing is ridiculously difficult.* It took me years of practice to get to a place where it's become more natural. But I still work on it, the same way I still go to the gym consistently.

Before I understood how to seesaw, I focused almost all my energy on building the business. It was just work, work, work all the time. I would come home with zero energy to give to my family. I wasn't present with my wife or children. I'd even cancel plans with family to meet with clients. Even then, despite valuing the other existing relationships I had, the time I put into my business prevented me from hanging out with cherished friends and seeing my parents.

Although I was highly focused on building Rastegar, it was to the detriment of many important personal relationships. I had outgrown certain relationships. We have a saying at Rastegar: "Either you are in, or you are in the way." There were plenty *in the way*. It's never fun, but sometimes you must make unapologetic adjustments to focus on the relationships that matter most.

It wasn't until I understood how to seesaw between home and work that I saw exponential improvement, which came from all directions. Maintaining focus at work kept me productive, engaged, and creative in providing solutions for my clients. Switching gears and giving that same focus at home brought happiness and fulfillment to my family. I also found productive ways to incorporate friends and parents back into my life.

> Knowing that I'm fully present with family and friends gives me the energy to continue seesawing my focus to where it's needed most.

Start small and take it slow. Don't expect yourself to succeed on day one. It will take time to get used to. Your mind will wander. You'll have days where you're exhausted and burnt out. You may lose concentration. Be sure not to beat yourself up. Start with small steps: go small to go far.

80/20 RULE

As you get into the swing of seesawing, apply the Pareto principle, otherwise known as the 80/20 rule. If you're unfamiliar with it, the principle states that the relationship between input and output is rarely balanced. According to the Pareto principle, approximately 20 percent of your efforts produce 80 percent of the results.[6]

When it comes to seesawing, we're aiming for excellence, not perfection—because guess what? Perfection is a lie. Aspire for excellence in all things—but especially in the small things when no one is watching.

If you're at home spending time with your family and an important call comes in, I don't expect you to ignore it. Handle the call, but don't let it completely derail the moment. This applies broadly. My nutrition is fairly on point these days, but I love pizza and French fries, so I will enjoy them on occasion. I'll enjoy a shot of tequila here and there, too. I'm still human. It's not like I'm trying to win the health award; I'm aiming to make healthy, productive decisions the *majority* of the time to better serve my team, my family, and my clients. Although this is about me, my life is not about me—it is for them. They are my *why*.

This reminds me of when Tony Robbins went out to dinner with Sage, who would later become his second wife. As the story goes, they went out to dinner together and shared an incredible meal. As a health advocate, he was interested in seeing what she would pick from the menu. To his delight, she picked a salad to start and fish for her main dish. Over dinner, they exchanged stories that revealed that they shared the same values. She meditated, she exercised, and she read books and was constantly seeking self-improvement. When the waiter came around to ask if they were interested in dessert, Tony immediately declined. "Oh no, thank you."

"I'll have a chocolate fudge sundae, please," Sage said.

Oh my God, Tony thought. *What is she doing? Doesn't she know how awful sugar is for you?*

It's as if his heart broke right then and there. When the waiter brought it out and placed it before her, Tony couldn't help himself. "I don't mean to be rude, but sugar is super, super bad for you."

"It's called living!" she replied, enjoying a heaping bite. He later said that moment changed his attitude toward life—that it's okay to *live*. She made quite the impression, and they married in 2001.

LEARN TO SAY NO, COMFORTABLY

A part of successfully seesawing is the ability to say no. Warren Buffett said, "The difference between successful people and really successful people is that really successful people say no to almost everything." That's because they're laser focused on their goals and don't want to get distracted by anything outside of reaching them. You must learn to be comfortable saying no.

Hey man, you want to go grab a beer? No.

You like tech, right? Are you interested in investing in my tech company? No.

I have a great business idea! Would you be interested in partnering? No.

I frequently receive proposals and requests to partner or invest in people's ideas and businesses. Some of them are even quite good, but that's not what I do, nor does it line up with my goals or aspirations, so I say no. I'm not implying for you to say no to everything, I'm saying your first instinct should be no, unless convinced otherwise, in order to keep you on *your path.*

Saying no, as you might suspect, was very uncomfortable at first. I'm a people pleaser by nature, and I didn't want to upset anyone or hurt their feelings. But, to reach my goal of becoming *ultra-successful,* I had to start being selective on how I spent my time and energy. If it didn't match with my goal, the answer became *no.*

Robert F. Smith once said, "The best part of being a billionaire is everyone takes your meeting." That's true, but I've learned firsthand that being a CEO and multimillionaire means being ultra-selective in which meetings *you* take and how you treat people.

MASTER YOUR FOCUS

"One reason so few of us achieve what we truly want is that we never direct our focus; we never concentrate our power. Most people dabble their way through life, never deciding to master anything in particular."

—TONY ROBBINS

It's as if Tony was speaking directly to me when he said the above quote. Once I learned how to seesaw my focus from one task to the next, that's when things finally started to fall into place and all aspects of my life improved.

My business grew and my relationships improved, which only added to my energy. I'm able to maintain healthy relationships and be successful in business not because I found a balance, but because I am laser-focused on whatever I'm doing in that moment.

Although you might not be able to physically see it, karma is real—which is the topic of our next chapter.

CHAPTER 9

KARMA IS REAL

"What you do speaks so loudly that I cannot hear what you say."
—RALPH WALDO EMERSON

In between college and law school, I worked at Paul Young Chevrolet in Laredo, Texas, selling used cars. Money was tight at the time. I was living paycheck to paycheck, which motivated me to be the best salesperson possible to maximize my commission. One day, a customer came in looking to buy a used car. He briefly told me what he had in mind and what he was willing to spend.

"I'm just looking for a simple, safe, and reliable car that can get me from point A to point B," he told me.

"I've got the perfect car for you. Follow me." I took him over to a blue Toyota Corolla at the end of the lot. "You can't get any more reliable than the Corolla. It's a global favorite and has a tremendous history of being safe—and it gets phenomenal gas mileage."

Honestly, I oversold the car. It was a bit outside of his budget, but my sheer determination to make the sale—I needed commissions to save money for law school—led to his decision to buy it. The deal went smoothly, and I couldn't have been more pleased: I got the commission that I desperately needed to pay for school and to cover bills for the month.

Unfortunately, the car didn't live up to the expectations I had enthused over, and he returned a week later. "You sold me a car that doesn't work!" he said angrily. "This is not what you sold me on!" He was exaggerating a bit, but his point was made, and it hit me hard.

My manager summoned the both of us into his office to resolve the issue. The client explained his frustration with the car's mechanics, the fuel light was broken, and the stereo had glitches, that he had found a better deal for a similar car elsewhere. He wanted his money back.

I was mortified. I wanted to crawl up in a hole. The onsite car mechanics never shared that the car had any issues, so I wasn't aware of its mechanical problems—which, thankfully, my manager vouched for. Even so, I took full responsibility.

"Sir, I am so sorry," I told him. "You have to believe me when I say I had no idea the car had issues. I figured the tank was just low on gas. I am utterly embarrassed. Please let me make this up to you. I'll tell you what: I'll waive my commission on another car from our lot. Please, I want to make this right."

My company honored his request and took the Corolla back. He ended up buying another car from me and, as promised, I waived my commission so he would get the best possible deal. Returning my commission put me in a precarious situation that month. But it was the right thing to do.

> Life's greatest lessons sometimes hurt. In fact, I'm convinced they always hurt. Instead of putting my client first, I put myself first—and the karma was instantaneous.

Instead of looking out for the best interest of my customer, I had tunnel vision on making a commission to pay my bills. I told myself that I would never do that again. And I haven't since, or at least never on purpose. Focusing on the client's best interest can sometimes seem counterintuitive, but it's right.

YOU GET WHAT YOU DESERVE

Even though most people associate the word karma with Buddhism or Hinduism, I separate it from religion. I am choosing to use the word karma because you likely understand the concept.

Lexico defines karma as "destiny or fate, following as effect from cause."[7] I personally view karma as cause and effect, as a scientific principle. The better you treat others, the better you treat yourself, the better the universe seems to reciprocate. But this also works in reverse. Putting me first and overselling the Corolla came back and bit me in the butt.

According to karma, I got exactly what I deserved.

Karma goes hand in hand with the law of attraction. Simply

put, the law of attraction states that you will attract into your life whatever you focus on. In other words, whatever you give your energy and attention to will come back to you.

Through the law of attraction, *like* attracts *like*, meaning similar things are attracted to one another. It's what our parents used to tell us as kids: If you're going to hang out with the troublemakers, then you'll become a troublemaker. Doctors hang out with other doctors. New parents hang out with other new parents. And so on. This extends into business, too. The employees you hire, or the vendors you contract with, or the clients you bring on will reflect who you are. We are defined by those closest to us.

Karma in Sanskrit means "act."[8] While the law of attraction suggests people's thoughts tend to attract similar results, karma can be applied in the same way, but to people's *actions*. You attract what you put out. The beauty in this process is that we can control it. That is the gift.

IT'S NOT ABOUT ME

A lot of our world is governed by self-interest. Overselling the car and experiencing that karma taught me that life is not just about me—a lesson I've learned several times over. It popped up again when I became a husband, when I became a father, and again when I became a business owner. The fact was that it wasn't just me anymore.

It's not about you. Yes, making money is a very important part of running a business, but not at the expense of other people. Overselling that car was the moment I promised myself that every deal moving forward, for the rest of my career, must benefit both parties. If it's not a win-win, then I won't do it.

IT'S NOT JUST ABOUT OTHERS EITHER

When we think of karma, we think about the golden rule: "Treat others the way you want to be treated." Although this is something everyone should live by, karma can also be applied to the actions you take for or against yourself.

Let's look at how you eat, for example. If you're mindlessly overeating junk food every day, karma will return to you in the form of poor health. If you have a negative inner voice that talks down to you and you don't talk back to it honestly, then ultimately all that you don't want will be exactly what you get: negativity, depression, and low self-esteem. If you're telling yourself you're going to do something, and then you don't do it, well, you're not cultivating good karma for yourself.

It's the same with business. As a CEO, how you show up and act serves as a role model to your staff. I'm the first to start work and the last to stop. I take care of my hygiene and appearance, I dress appropriately, I take care of my health mentally, physically, and spiritually, and by setting the expectations for myself, I subconsciously elevate the expectations of those around me.

HOW TO CULTIVATE GOOD KARMA

The easiest way to cultivate good karma is to simply be a good human being and practice treating others well.

Duh, you might be thinking. Sounds simple enough, but common sense isn't so common, and life is complicated and emotional.

You already know my creed—my guide for how to treat people and how to live life—and I work on it every day. I analyze it and point out what I did wrong so I can continuously improve.

Cultivating good karma is about mastery. What leads to mastery? A practice. When I use the word *practice*, here, I'm using it as a noun, not a verb. Like a law practice or a medical practice, it's an ongoing event that you continue doing. And a practice is goalless. It's a lifestyle. You show up, every day, and do the work. It's who you are and *what* you are; the actions you engage in are byproducts of your practice.

There's a great dichotomy here: yes, we need to have goals that can be concretely reached, but we also need to have a practice that we do regardless of a goal. Call it a process. Many talented artists call it their "craft."

With a goal, you know where you're going. When I talk about practice, I'm talking about the things you do that are embedded in your daily living—it's who you are. If you're a basketball player, for example, you shoot free throws every day. It's a part of your life. You're not shooting free throws because you want to score eighty points in the next game; it's bigger than that. If you're a musician, you're playing music every day, experimenting with different keys and chords, not always aiming to write a song or produce a record, but it's because maintaining your skills is part of who you are. It's something that you live by. It's a creed, a ritual. It's sacred and eternal.

Your creed is how you should treat everything. It's an always thing.

It all comes back to *you*. That is the good news and the bad news—cause and effect resulting from self-reliance.

TREATING PEOPLE RIGHT

"Not only is there often a right or wrong, but what goes around does come around. Karma exists."

—DONALD VAN DE MARK

I'm grateful for the failure that led to the embarrassing lesson in karma on the used car lot that happened when I was very young. I'm also grateful that it was an $800 problem and not an $8 billion problem. It seems as life gets longer and we get further along in our careers, the problems and lessons become more expensive. If you're lucky, the failures will come early.

More importantly, I took that failure and the lessons learned from it and applied them to Rastegar many, many years later. Its foundation is rooted in treating people right. We put our clients first, we treat our employees like family, and we put long-term value over short-term profit. We always plan for the long game, with both people and opportunities. When I took my own self-interest out of the equation, it led to happier relations, happier employees, happier customers, and a happier me.

When you are willing to forego your own interests to help someone else, they know they can rely on you. I don't need to be right. I just want the best answer that we can discern from the information available. Karma will reward you disproportionately well. Something magical happens when interests are authentically aligned. Doing right by someone that hurts you is also wrong. It must be mutual, fair, and congruent. We aren't martyrs. We're in search of those who share common core values and mutual self-interest.

The gentleman who bought the car ended up becoming a lifelong client for Paul Young Chevrolet. Even after I stopped working there, he bought several more cars over the years. Even though I screwed up the first sale, I made up for it in a way that left a positive enough impression on him to be loyal to the dealership for years afterward.

Now, that's some good karma.

CHAPTER 10

YOU HAVE TO BELIEVE IN SOMETHING TO BE GREAT

"Take the first step in faith. You don't have to see the whole staircase, just take the first step."

—DR. MARTIN LUTHER KING JR.

I loved watching sports as a kid. But despite how much I loved basketball and baseball, I really sucked at sports. Even as a wrestler, I felt more like a punching bag.

My childhood is riddled with embarrassing sports-related failures. For example, when I played peewee football, I once scored a touchdown for the other team. Similarly, my baseball coach somehow thought it would be a good idea for me to pitch in a live game—which led to me failing to get the ball to the plate for three straight innings. I wanted to be athletic, but I just didn't have it in me back then. Today I train not for sports, but for the Olympics of life.

My embarrassing childhood failures didn't end with sports, either. Baba wanted me to play violin, but I sucked at that, too, as evidenced by my always being placed in last chair. My speech impediment didn't help, either. It was so bad that my teachers thought I had a learning disability. All these failures ate away at my self-confidence, not that there was a lot there in the first place.

After my parents' divorce, I lived with my mom until I was about ten years old. Starting from sixth grade, I then lived with Baba until I graduated high school. My dad attended law school at the time, so we lived in his school's student housing, which put me in the Highland Park School District—one of the richest school districts in Texas. That might sound nice, but we were *not* affluent. I felt intimidated by attending a school with a bunch of rich kids, because I wasn't one of them. This fostered an intense insecurity regarding money and gave me great anxiety.

Even though we didn't have the disposable income my peers had, Baba did everything in his power to provide. He would do anything to help me blend in (like buy me a brand-new car when I got my license, for example). But nothing he could do addressed the deep, internal insecurity I had with money, and it showed up in school in a variety of ways. Not performing as an athlete was one of them (coupled with still being haunted by my embarrassing childhood athletic endeavors).

"Baba, I suck at sports," I said one day.

"What? What do you mean you suck at sports? Your grandfather was a gold medalist. You're a great athlete. It's in your DNA."

"No, Baba. Every time I try to play a sport, I embarrass myself. I really suck."

"Don't you ever say that again. You can excel at anything you focus on consistently."

After a minute of silence, he said in his thick accent, "You know what? Let's go shoot some hoops."

Coming from my dad, this was a lovely fatherly gesture since he wasn't into sports himself. We bonded over basketball. Even though I believed I wasn't any good, he'd tell me otherwise. He'd point out the excellent control I had over the ball as I pushed through his body toward the basket. He commented on my ability to move quickly on my feet as I took command of the court. He applauded the concentration I'd exerted with free throws, nailing more than I missed.

Seeing my potential, he called upon his own mother, my grandma "Mozzy," and she, ironically enough, became my one-on-one basketball coach. Mozzy didn't know anything about basketball; nevertheless, she was invaluable at helping me drill down the fundamentals. She'd come over and she'd hand me the ball and instruct me to practice my layups and three-pointers, and then we'd run a series of drills. My uncle Sahel, my dad's youngest brother, also was and still is an incredible athlete. He was an unbelievable basketball player himself, and would come over to play with me, too.

Soon enough, my skills improved, and my confidence grew—not only in the game, but in myself. When it was just me and Baba on the court, I was incredible, which gave me the boost I needed to play against other neighborhood kids. They organized pick-up games at the local park a few times a week, and I mustered enough courage to participate. After the first game, my confidence grew. Baba was right: I *was* good. On most occasions, I competed against those much older than me—some were even college-aged—and I held my own even though I was only five-foot-two at the time.

Seeing how much I loved the game, and witnessing my skills improving, my dad encouraged me to try out for the sixth-grade basketball team. "You're super talented, Ari. You're going to be a starter."

But when I went to try out, my anxiety set in and I felt mentally paralyzed. I compared myself to the other players, most of whom were taller and had better basketball sneakers, which eroded my confidence. I felt inadequate being around my wealthy peers. All I could think about was how I was the poorest kid in the room, and that showed up in my performance—which was downright abysmal. As soon as someone passed me the ball, I froze on the spot, as if someone had put crazy glue on my shoes. When I finally snapped out of it, I ran the wrong way down the court (not again!). I missed every shot I took. Everyone laughed and made fun of me.

Needless to say, I didn't make the team. I was so traumatized that I never tried out for the basketball team again, despite my absolute love of the game. In fact, I was so upset that I developed a disdain for sports in general. And even though I had watched sports like football, baseball, and basketball religiously before, I stopped watching games altogether. To this day, I only watch sports if it's a pro friend of mine, or pure greatness like Serena Williams, Messi, Brady, LeBron, or the like.

> I had a lot of things going against me as a kid—all of which stemmed from insecurity and not believing in myself. You can have all the innate ability and the talent in the world, but if you don't believe in yourself, none of that matters.

FAITH VS. BELIEF

According to Lexico, faith is defined as "the complete trust or confidence in someone or something."[9]

Belief is defined as "something one accepts as true or real, or a firmly held belief."

Faith is the connection into belief. Even though you may not see the next step, knowing that it's there is where belief enters. Belief is the bridge to accomplishing our goals. Until faith turns into belief, it's not tangible. We are governed by our beliefs. Our actions are the sum of what we believe to be true.

Just like karma, this has nothing to do with religion. A lot of people use the words faith and religion interchangeably. To me, they are different. Although your faith can certainly be associated with religion, it doesn't have to be. Faith can be applied to yourself, your family, your business, and a multitude of other things.

If you have faith in a religion, this concept may be easier for you to grasp since you believe in a higher power—someone or something greater. The key is to transmute it into what you want.

If we look at the history of very wealthy people, a lot of them were pious and religious. They had faith in something other than themselves. When building your business, you must believe—in your team, your clients, your product, all the above. It can't and shouldn't just be about you.

There's a classic story about John D. Rockefeller being late for a train that was supposed to take him to an important business meeting with Cornelius Vanderbilt for a life-changing opportunity. Rockefeller was normally very punctual and very pious. However, the train crashed, and being late saved his life. After that experience, Rockefeller believed that his destiny was to do something great. He was right because he made himself right.

HOW TO BUILD YOUR FAITH

If you want to build faith, it's like building a muscle. You can't just go to the gym, lift some weights, and expect to be ripped the next day. You must commit to a regimen or ritual. You must be consistent. You must start small and ease into it. Let's say you start with twenty-pound dumbbells. After consistently going to the gym three days in that first week, you can increase the weight when you're ready. Your body grew stronger and can handle the heavier load. You'd then increase it again. The more consistent you are, the more confident you will be in moving to heavier weights. Don't fear going slow;

be scared of not moving. The power of consistent growth is grossly underestimated.

Faith and belief work in the same way. They are like muscles you need to train. You must do the work to build faith and then convert it to belief. When it becomes a belief, that's when you start to see results.

In the same vein, the more muscle you have, the harder it is to lose it. Of course, if you stop training over a long period of time, you will eventually lose most of it, but after putting in the time and effort in building the muscle in the first place, your body takes longer to atrophy. Once you get back on it, your neurons, brain, and muscles remember, and your body more readily bounces back.

The same can be said for faith and belief.

If you're new to developing faith, you're not alone. You might be asking where to begin, or how to build faith in yourself.

As previously mentioned, one easy way to start is to write down your goals, exclaim them aloud, passionately, emphatically, and powerfully. With enough practice and repetition, your mind starts to believe it.

This works the other way, too. If you continually talk down to yourself, your inner voice then destroys any faith and replaces it with negative emotions that drain your energy. You want to choose positivity, gratitude, faith, and other elevated emotions.

Bill Gates became a billionaire at thirty-one years old. When asked what the secret was to this success, he replied: "There's no secret. I worked really hard on my idea to get it as good as I could, and then knocked on door after door. I ended up showing my idea to 1,200 people. Nine hundred said no. Thirty took a serious look. And eleven made me a multi-millionaire." He believed in what he was offering and that it would take off—it was just a matter of getting it in front of the right people that needed the service.

When I first wrote down my goal of becoming a billionaire, I didn't know how it would happen (and it hasn't happened yet). I didn't have a plan. Everyone viewed my goal as out-landish and unrealistic, quite frankly impossible, but that's where faith stepped in. I believed it would happen, someway, somehow.

All you need to know is the *what* and the *why*. The *how* is none of your business. That's faith.

MIND MOVIES

The book *Becoming Supernatural* introduced me to the company (and concept) of Mind Movies, which is an extraordinary method to review, internalize, and ultimately accomplish your goals.

I'm sure you're familiar with a vision board: it's usually a poster board with a collage of goal images that serve as a source of inspiration and motivation. Mind Movies is a twenty-first century vision board in movie format. Mind

Movies takes your vision board and transforms it into a fun, digital video filled with the same images and affirmations, with motivating music. It's a way to activate and use more of your senses. In addition to serving to remind you of your goals and aspirations, it's a great way to build your faith in yourself and your future. I watch my Mind Movie almost every day, once in the morning and once before bedtime.

Depending on my stress levels throughout the day, I'll give the video a watch anytime I'm feeling down and my faith takes a dip, or when I'm excited and feel the goal nearing. Whenever I watch it, I engage elevated emotion and picture myself reaching all the goals presented. The video helps me visualize what it would be like to attain them. With the motivational music and the affirmations, watching the video always gives me that extra pep in my step. It fills me with hope and confidence, which restores the faith I have in myself to continue working toward my goals.

I took this idea of visualization and faith-building a step further and dedicated a room in my office that I call the Dream Lab. The entire room, about three hundred square feet, is covered in inspirational quotes, pictures, and all my goals. There's even a TV that plays my Mind Movies on repeat. Whenever I get discouraged, unfocused, or a bit defeated, I'll go sit in my dream lab to remind myself of my *why*. I'll read the quotes and speak my goals out loud, look at the pictures, and then visualize them coming true. It's a full-scale immersion that restores and maintains my faith momentum.

Now, obviously you don't have to take it to this extreme. You can easily do something similar to achieve the same effect.

Print out your goals or write them down on post-it notes and leave them around your house. I prefer to handwrite goals; it feels more tangible. Print out pictures of things that represent your goals and strategically place them so you will see them every day. Tape them to the ceiling above your bed so they're the first thing you see every morning and the last thing you see before lights out. Put those sticky notes on the mirror in the bathroom so you can read them while you're brushing your teeth.

Be creative and try to engage all your senses. Watch videos, listen to inspirational music, look at photos, and put your body into it when reading your goals out loud. The more senses involved, the deeper your faith will cultivate, which expedites the time you'll transmute your goals into beliefs.

FIND YOUR DREAM PARTNERS

Faith is fragile, so you need to surround yourself with staunch supporters who love and believe in you fully—and I mean with a no-holds-barred, undying, unconditional type of love and support. What you want are *dream partners*.

A dream partner is someone you can share your wildest dreams with, and because their belief in you is unwavering, they will never shoot you down. In fact, they'll double down and make you feel like you are a superhero.

When making audacious goals, it's easy to get discouraged when others can't see what you see. Nothing deflates a dream like having your significant other or family member say it's silly, or your best friend call it unrealistic. That's why it's important to keep the wildest of dreams to yourself and only share them with a very few, selected people—your dream partners.

I used to share my ideas freely but quickly learned it was detrimental to my self-esteem and confidence. People called me all sorts of names, but the looks and smirks were the most painful. They'd immediately shoot down my ideas. I've even had mentors who love and support me say that my aspirations were ridiculous. My dreams were too monstrous for them. They couldn't wrap their head around how I would accomplish them. In their view, they were unthinkable.

Fair enough. It's not like they were wrong—my ideas *were* too much for *them*. But it just goes to show you that they didn't truly know *me*. What can I say? I'm a dreamer, and dreamers possess an innate ability to see further. But dreamers should also expect opposition and believe they will be successful anyway—and your dream partners are a part of that equation. Einstein said, "Great spirits have always encountered violent opposition from mediocre minds." Harsh? Yes, but true.

One of my dearest friends, Dustin Mehaffey, is my main dream partner. No matter what I dream up, he always believes in me. Every time I presented an idea, no matter how wild or outlandish, he expressed nothing but support and enthusiasm. Dustin always one-upped me: I aimed for a jet, and he insisted on a C-130 that could carry a small village. Never once did he discourage me or try to bring me down from the clouds. Never once did he try to convince me to go after something he thought was more attainable. Never once did he say, "No, Ari. You can't do that."

No idea was unfathomable. Everything was always on the table. Dream partners jump in to help in any capacity. No matter how absurd my proposals or objectives were, they always had my back and were willing to do whatever it took to make them a reality. They are my dream partners because they've always dreamt with me. Then I got back to work, refueled.

Obviously, some of my ideas worked out and most didn't, as is life. My dream partners and I would work on them incognito, putting in the work to make them happen. The ones that failed were abandoned, or I'd readjust them to something that would work. Agility is key. Stay focused on the goal but be agile and adaptable in the approach. Once I'd gain some traction and position it on a solid path forward, that's when I'd come out publicly and share it with the rest of the team—and the naysayers. At that point, thanks in part to my dream partners, I'd built enough resilience and belief in myself and the project that I could shake off the skeptics. After all, they didn't know any better. Most were just sorry they'd given up on their own dreams. Sad, but true.

Dustin strengthened the confidence I have in myself, not only in business but also as a person. We still have "dream sessions" to this day. It's a ritual. Each of my dream partner's unfaltering belief in me only fortified my belief in myself, and as such, my partners have helped me to build the incredible life that I had first only seen in my head.

THE FAITH TO START MY BUSINESS

In 2015, before starting Rastegar, I worked for a company in

New York that asked me to do something that violated my creed. I just couldn't do it, nor could I live with myself to continue working at a place that expected me to go against my code. So, I quit on the spot. As it usually goes with these situations, timing was not great, to say the least. Kellie was pregnant, and we were living paycheck to paycheck. We barely made rent for our little apartment each month. When I came home and told her I quit my job, she almost went into labor right then and there. Although the timing was horrendous, I wasn't willing to put my integrity on the line. The need for money cost too much to potentially compromise my integrity.

I needed to figure out what to do—and fast. Looking for guidance, I went to one of my mentors, a long-time wealthy Houston investor and dear friend who has since passed away. I explained my dilemma to him. "Stop working for someone else," he said. "Why don't you start your own company?"

"Start my own company?" I replied with a laugh. "I don't think I'm ready. Besides, I don't have the capital to launch a business."

"Well, when you're ready to grow up and do it, call me. Maybe I can help."

Well, okay then.

So, I just went for it. It was like an invisible nudge from my higher self. I called him, we came up with a plan, and with his guidance, what is now Rastegar was born.

In that previous moment of uncertainty about providing for

my family, my faith had certainly dipped. I hadn't believed in myself and my abilities to start my own company. The faith this mentor and dear friend had in me—and his belief that I could do it—reversed that dip and elevated me to the highest of highs. In fact, he changed my life. He believed in me more than I believed in myself.

NOTHING IS IMPOSSIBLE

"You must find the place inside yourself where nothing is impossible."

—DEEPAK CHOPRA

Having faith that then turns into belief is often that extra element you need for things to work out. If I truly believed in myself as a kid, I would have made the basketball team in sixth grade. But building faith into belief is like building a muscle: you must do it consistently.

I've built my faith and belief muscles so much over the years that whenever failure rears its head nowadays, I have the strength to immediately pivot and find a better solution. I spend 5 percent of my time on the problem and 95 percent on the solution. With the right core values and mindset, things always tend to work out because my faith and belief muscles are now strong.

What we once thought was impossible, with enough work, then seems probable—and eventually, it becomes inevitable.

CONCLUSION

"You are essentially who you create yourself to be and all that occurs in your life is the result of your own making."

—STEPHEN RICHARDS

To honor my grandfather, the doors to the Rastegar office have his name, my father's name, and my ancestors' names on them to remind me that they're watching. Every day, I'm reminded to stay true, stay focused, and aspire to be my best self, my authentic self. If I can give my best to the company, then the company can give its best to the world. So can you.

This is the potential that I hope you see: to contribute to your community and to make a better world. This is what makes all our failures worth it—because those failures taught us how to measure success not only as business people, but as human beings.

So, what does success look like to you? How will you measure your worth?

Only you can set the standards you live by. Only you can embrace the gift of failure, grow into the person you were meant to be, and leave a lasting impact on the world around you. When you focus on improving yourself, the benefits will trickle down to all aspects of your life. Everything is analogous.

Since this is an ongoing, never-ending journey, you should constantly be evolving, learning to be agile, and reinventing yourself. It will never stop—I surely don't plan to. When you stop learning, you stop developing and you stop growing.

START SMALL

In anything you do, be sure to start small. Those audacious life goals are composed of moment-to-moment smaller accomplishments. It's harder to go small because it takes humility, vulnerability, and courage. Master the short game before the long. Conquer one superb push-up before doing twenty lame ones. Learning how to seesaw and focus on the task at hand and complete each step toward living the life you desire is the way to achieve greatness. Start with a one-minute meditation. Go to the gym one day a week for a few weeks, and then increase that to two. Make these goals so ridiculously practical and attainable that there's no reason not to do them. That's how you build momentum.

Don't get too excited and lay out a whole series of changes you want to implement *right now*, because that's simply not effective. When you try to do too much at once, you'll inevitably get overwhelmed, which will lead you to not doing anything at all. You'll feel bad about yourself, which is discouraging, and then you'll quit before you even got started.

Once you start conquering those micro goals, you'll build your confidence and your faith, which will eventually grow into belief. You'll tap into elevated emotions, like passion and love. The more passion and love you feel in yourself, the more motivated you will be to keep going. This only further builds momentum.

It's never too late to start, regardless of your age, your background, or your expertise. Success doesn't discriminate against age or experience. It only discriminates against those who don't try. There are more success stories from people who decided to change their sails later in life and found amazing success, more than you could imagine. For example, Harland Sanders, also known as Colonel Sanders, the original founder of KFC, franchised his fast-food chain at the age of sixty-two and would later sell the company for several million dollars.

Actor Ronald Reagan was fifty-four when he announced he was running for governor of California in 1965. I'd say his political career worked out well for him since he became the fortieth president of the United States in 1981. Similarly, actor Arnold Schwarzenegger left a successful career in Hollywood and became the governor of California in 2003 at the age of fifty-six.

Warren Buffet's net worth in 2020 was estimated to be $85 billion, but he made 99 percent of his wealth *after* sixty years old. Think about that: *99 percent*. He played the long game, and I implore you to do the same.

The first step is having the willingness to start. As Deborah Day said, "Recognizing that you are not where you want to be is a starting point to begin changing your life."

THE GIFT OF FAILURE

Failure comes in many forms. It can come in a failed business, in failing health, or in failing to represent yourself well and strengthen relationships with those around you. These are some of the failures that defined me. From these, I learned to plan for the unexpected, to take care of my health and well-being first, and to be relentlessly mindful of how I present myself to others so that I can turn first impressions into long-term connections. From each of these lessons, and many others, I learned how to be a better person—and ultimately a better leader and entrepreneur.

Being an entrepreneur is not for the faint of heart. You will experience failure, and that's okay. Failures are gifts, as long as you apply introspection and take the time to learn from them. As Maxime Lagacé once said, "There's meaning in every failure. Find it." That's the gift.

Instead of focusing on disappointment or finding someone or something to blame, we must look within. We must understand what happened, why it happened, and what strategies we can implement for ourselves to avoid similar failures in the future. Failing is going to happen; expect it and embrace it; it is part of the process. It's most of the process. It's messy, it's not linear, and it hurts. But it's worth it. Please be a bigger person than me and enjoy it. You must fail to become successful, because honestly, success teaches you nothing. In fact, success makes you arrogant. That's why I hope you fail a lot. Failure offers you the opportunity to examine what you did and learn from it so you can move forward humbly but confidently.

You have greatness within you, you just have to tap into it—but that falls on you and only you. Accept responsibility for your life. Know that it is you, it is always you.

I hope the stories and insights I shared benefit you as you take responsibility for your life and pursue your own never-ending journey of self-improvement. I encourage you to share this book with other wild dreamers so they, too, can benefit. I would also love to hear from you. Email me at TheGift@RastegarProperty.com. I want to hear about your failures, your successes, and your discoveries. I want to hear how working on yourself has improved your business. I want to hear about how you are changing the world and if I can help. I will read the emails myself and truly cherish them.

Success is not what you get in life; it's about who you become through each gift of failure.

FURTHER LEARNING LIST

BOOKS AND ESSAYS

Daniel Coyle, *The Talent Code: Greatness Isn't Born. It's Grown. Here's How.*

Raymond Dalio, *Principles: Life and Work*

Joe Dispenza, *Becoming Supernatural: How Common People Are Doing the Uncommon*

Pete Egoscue, *Pain Free: A Revolutionary Method for Stopping Chronic Pain*

Ralph Waldo Emerson, "Self-Reliance" from *Essays*

Martin Greenfield with Wynton Hall, *Measure of a Man: From Auschwitz Survivor to Presidents' Tailor*

Tim Grover with Shari Lesser Wenk, *Relentless: From Good to Great to Unstoppable*

Napoleon Hill, *Think and Grow Rich*

Wim Hof, *The Wim Hof Method: Activate Your Full Human Potential*

Tony Hsieh, *Delivering Happiness: A Path to Profits, Passion, and Purpose*

Ariana Huffington, *The Sleep Revolution: Transforming Your Life, One Night at a Time*

Gary Keller and Jay Papasan, *The One Thing: The Surprisingly Simple Truth Behind Extraordinary Results*

Matthew McConaughey, *Greenlights*

Jacob Rosenstein, *Defy Aging: Make the Rest of Your Life the Best of Your Life*

Lauren Handel Zander, *Maybe It's You: Cut the Crap. Face Your Fears. Love Your Life.*

Intelligent Change, *The Five-Minute Journal*

VIDEOS

Brené Brown, "The Power of Vulnerability," TEDxHouston 2010, www.ted.com/talks/brene_brown_the_power_of_vulnerability

Amy Cuddy, "Your Body Language May Shape Who You Are," TEDGlobal 2012, www.ted.com/talks/amy_cuddy_your_body_language_may_shape_who_you_are

Lauren Zander, "No One Is Coming to Save You! Becoming Your Own Hero," TEDxAmsterdamWomen 2011, www.youtube.com/watch?v=_ntKfkGnvMA

PRODUCTS AND SERVICES

The Egoscue Method, www.egoscue.com

Green Vibrance, www.vibranthealth.com

The Handel Method, www.handelgroup.com

Inner U, www.inneru.coach

SciLife Science VitaYears Multivitamin, www.scilifebiosciences.com

The Wim Hof Method mobile app, www.wimhofmethod.com/wim-hof-method-mobile-app

GREAT QUOTES ON FAILURE

"Many of life's failures are people who did not realize how close they were to success when they gave up."

—THOMAS EDISON

"Even if you fail at your ambitious thing, it's very hard to fail completely."

—LARRY PAGE

"Failure and invention are inseparable twins."

—JEFF BEZOS

"I can accept failure. Everyone fails at something. But I can't accept not trying."

—MICHAEL JORDAN

"With engineering, I view this year's failure as next year's opportunity to try it again. Failures are not something to be avoided. You want to have them happen as quickly as you can so you can make progress rapidly."

—GORDON MOORE

"Failure is an event, not a person. Yesterday ended last night."

—ZIG ZIGLAR

"In my experience, each failure contains the seeds of your next success—if you are willing to learn from it."

—PAUL ALLEN

"There's no such thing as failure. There are only results."

—TONY ROBBINS

"In a world that's changing really quickly, the only strategy that is guaranteed to fail is not taking risks."

—MARK ZUCKERBERG

"If things are not failing, you are not innovating enough."

—ELON MUSK

NOTES

1   "The Profound Life Lesson of Oxygen Masks," Human Unlimited, accessed February 4, 2022, https://www.humanunlimited.com/blogs/blog/20030915-the-profound-life-lesson-of-oxygen-masks.

2   Kurt Badenhausen, "The Highest-Paid Athletes of the Decade: Mayweather, Ronaldo and LeBron Dominate," *Forbes*, December 23, 2019, https://www.forbes.com/sites/kurtbadenhausen/2019/12/23/the-highest-paid-athletes-of-the-decade-mayweatherronaldo-lebron-score/?sh=6fddea0a72d9.

3   Quench USA, Inc., "Nearly 80 Percent of Working Americans Say They Don't Drink Enough Water: Quench Survey," PR Newswire, June 19, 2018, https://www.prnewswire.com/news-releases/nearly-80-percent-of-working-americans-say-they-dont-drink-enough-water-quench-survey-300668537.html.

4   "Vitamin & Supplement Manufacturing in the US – Market Size 2005–2027," IBISWorld, last modified October 24, 2021, https://www.ibisworld.com/industry-statistics/market-size/vitamin-supplement-manufacturing-united-states/.

5   Keld Jensen, "Intelligence Is Overrated: What You Really Need to Succeed," *Forbes*, April 12, 2012, https://www.forbes.com/sites/keldjensen/2012/04/12/intelligence-is-overrated-what-you-really-need-to-succeed/?sh=6e5d7e05b6d2.

6   The Investopedia Team, "Pareto Principle," Investopedia, last modified December 25, 2020, https://www.investopedia.com/terms/p/paretoprinciple.asp.

7   *Lexico*, s.v. "Karma," accessed February 24, 2022, https://www.lexico.com/en/definition/karma.

8   "Karma."

9   *Lexico*, s.v. "Faith," accessed February 24, 2022, https://www.lexico.com/en/definition/faith.